A Supervisor's
Guide to

You Said Yes!

A Supervisor's
Guide to

You Said Yes!

How to Recruit,
Train, and Sustain
Literacy Tutors

Patricia A. Oliver
Mary L. Wheeler

Heinemann
Portsmouth, NH

Heinemann
A division of Reed Elsevier Inc.
361 Hanover Street
Portsmouth, NH 03801–3912
www.heinemann.com

Offices and agents throughout the world

Library of Congress Cataloging-in-Publication Data
Oliver, Patricia A.
    A supervisor's guide to you said yes! : how to recruit, train, and sustain
literacy tutors / Patricia A. Oliver, Mary L. Wheeler.
        p. cm.
    Includes bibliographical references and index.
    ISBN 0-325-00809-4 (alk. paper)
    1. Reading (Elementary).   2. Reading—Remedial teaching.   3. Tutors and
tutoring.   4. Literacy programs.   5. Volunteer workers in education.   I. Wheeler, Mary L.
II. Title.

LB1573.O53 2005
371.1'124—dc22   2005020043

Editor: Lois Bridges
Production: Patricia Adams
Typesetter: Publishers' Design and Production Services, Inc.
Cover design: Jenny Jensen Greenleaf
Manufacturing: Jamie Carter

Printed in the United States of America on acid-free paper

09   08   07   06   05   VP   1   2   3   4   5

To Judy Wallis.
Thank you for your endless
support and continuous inspiration.
You are *our* gardener.

CONTENTS

When looking at the ingredients on the label of a can, the one that is listed *first* is the main ingredient. Even though we mention many people in these acknowledgments, we want our readers to know that they are *all* the main ingredient behind this effort. No worthy thing happens in life unless someone has an idea and pursues it. Empowering literacy volunteers to work with our students is such a worthy thing. There are so many "someones" we need to recognize as this book becomes a reality.

Without the vision of Judy Wallis, language arts coordinator for Spring Branch Independent School District in Houston, Texas, and Lynnda Butorka, her administrative assistant, none of these materials would ever have taken this form. Without the Spring Branch Education Foundation, none of this effort would have been funded. Without the support and enthusiasm of our administrators and fellow school improvement specialists, we could have lost our momentum. And without the wisdom, expertise, patience, and professional heart of our editor Lois Bridges and production editor Patty Adams, we would have been lost. We lift up and salute the inspirational senior citizens from Memorial City Terrace Retirement Home and Pines Presbyterian Church who have been our role models for our literacy tutoring programs. Tom Potts, our charter senior tutor, helped to plant the seeds of using senior citizens in the school as tutors as he coined the phrase that his generation is our largest "untapped resource." Sometimes the children on the fringe who seem to skirt around the edges of understanding just need the wisdom of and relationship with an older person who cares about them to help them become at ease with the written word. And finally, we applaud our husbands and children who have believed in us and have watched these books hatch from dinner conversations to a bound reality. Long live literacy!

Take a moment and picture a dedicated and well-meaning volunteer literacy tutor sitting next to a young reader. The volunteer leans so close to the student their heads almost touch. A simple, predictable book with colorful matching illustrations lays open on the table in front of them. It seems like a perfect scene. But you notice the student's hands remain quietly in his lap as the tutor points to the words. The student hesitates and you hear the tutor quickly supply the unknown word. And then it happens: You hear the tutor say, "Don't look at the pictures!"

You cringe just a little because you know the teacher has been working with this same student in the classroom. But in the classroom, his teacher is moving him toward becoming an *independent self-determining* reader. She expects him to turn the pages and point to the words on the page. She watches as he searches the illustrations for clues that might help create meaning. He rarely looks at the teacher to supply an unknown word. When he hesitates, his teacher gently prompts him, "Check the picture. What would make sense? Say the first sound. What would sound right?" In the classroom, he hears an entirely different message than he hears with his tutor.

The tutor is not deliberately trying to confuse the student, but she does need some training in what to do with a student before, during, and after reading. In other words, the volunteer needs the support of a *knowledgeable other* just as much as the student.

ᘓ ᘓ ᘓ

With the ever-increasing need for supporting struggling readers and the ever-decreasing school budgets, more and more schools are looking to volunteers to provide additional support. It is a delicate matter though because placing a student who is already confused about the complexities of reading and writing with an untrained volunteer may cause more problems than solutions.

According to the *No Child Left Behind Act*, "Improving the reading skills of children is a top priority for leaders at all levels of government and business, as well as for parents, teachers and countless citizens who *volunteer* at reading programs across the nation." (Italics added by authors.) Volunteer tutors are not certified teachers and should not be expected to take the place of a classroom teacher. But with explicit training from a qualified supervisor, it is possible to supplement classroom instruction with effective one-to-one tutoring by a volunteer literacy tutor (Cohen, Kulik, and Kulik 1982; Juel 1996).

So how do you recruit, train, and support your volunteer tutors? How do you create an effective literacy tutoring program? First, you need some basic information about what is needed to ensure an effective tutoring program. There are several key factors that should be considered (Wasik 1997, 1998; Wasik and Slavin 1993).

- A certified reading specialist needs to supervise tutors.

- Tutors must have ongoing training and feedback.

- Tutoring sessions should be structured and contain several components such as familiar reading, word analysis, writing, and introduction of new stories.

- Tutoring should be intensive and consistent.

- Tutors should have access to quality materials.

- Assessment of students needs to be ongoing.

- Schools need to ensure that tutors attend regularly.

- Tutoring should be coordinated with classroom instruction.

These key factors make one point clear—someone in each school needs to take charge of the volunteer program. Research concludes that the key person in any tutoring program is the facilitator or supervisor (Pinnell and Fountas 1997). The supervisor doesn't necessarily have to be a certified reading specialist. But, the supervisor should be someone who is knowledgeable about the reading development of students and passionate about no child being left on the fringes.

This book (and its companion book *You Said Yes! Support Materials for Volunteer Literacy Tutors*) lays the groundwork for creating an effective volunteer literacy tutoring program that meets the demands of the National Reading Panel and *No Child Left Behind Act*. It provides information for supervisors and tutors that addresses the five skills identified by research as critical to early reading success (National Reading Panel 2000):

1. **Phonemic awareness.** The ability to hear and identify sounds in spoken words.

2. **Phonics.** The relationship between the letters of written language and the sounds of spoken language.

3. **Fluency.** The capacity to read text accurately and quickly.

4. **Vocabulary.** The words students must know to communicate effectively.

5. **Comprehension.** The ability to understand and gain meaning from what has been read.

This book includes the theoretical and practical information needed to build a successful, research-based volunteer literacy tutoring program. With concise and explicit information on how to recruit, train, and sustain volunteers, this book reads like a Betty Crocker cookbook. The directions are simple, easy to follow, and logical. Basing your volunteer literacy tutoring program on a detailed map of the road ahead will make the trip much easier. Supervisors, tutors, and teachers will enjoy this journey!

A Supervisor's Guide to

You Said **Yes!**

CHAPTER 1

Get Ready, Get Set, Go!

Now that you know where you want to go, let's focus for a minute on how to lay the groundwork for an effective volunteer literacy tutoring program. From the beginning, base your volunteer program on the three *Cs—commitment, communication,* and *community*. When the following volunteers, teachers, and administrators feel like a part of the program they will automatically give you the cheerleaders you need. Success depends on inviting the key people to be partners in the initial planning. You may not need all of the following members on your campus volunteer literacy team, but tapping into the *right* people will build a solid support system. These key people are:

- the reading specialist or literacy coach

- administrator(s) and administrative assistant(s)

- classroom teachers who are interested and will support literacy tutors

- the school librarian who can provide books and other resources

- specialists who can contribute to training and supervision

- a counselor (He or she often knows individuals or groups that might be interested in becoming volunteers.)

- an office staff member (This person is critical since she will be the first one to greet your volunteers and transmit messages.)

- a PTA and/or community volunteer liaison

Once a campus volunteer literacy team has been established, several decisions should be made before you begin to recruit and train your literacy volunteers. Remember, the more planning you do early on, the more effective and productive your literacy tutoring program will be. Here are a few suggestions.

1. *Decide who will be responsible for the training and supervision of the tutoring program.* This person should be a reading specialist, literacy coach, or at the very least a person who has a strong background in reading. This person must have a flexible enough schedule to allow her to provide the necessary support. If possible, more than one person can be responsible for supervising the tutors.

2. *Brainstorm where you think you might find volunteers.* Look for volunteers at churches, retirement homes, or community colleges—the list is longer than you think.

3. *Establish the time commitment expected of tutors.* This is critical! Tutors need to know how long the tutoring sessions will be and the minimum number of hours expected to tutor each week. While there are several ways to set up a volunteer literacy tutoring program, this book focuses on two models (see Chapter 2).

4. *Clarify your expectations for the tutors.* Will they just read with students or be able to reach for pencils, paper, magnetic letters, or erasable boards when the need arises? A clear understanding of expectations will help determine how much and what training will be needed.

5. *Be conscious of the school budgets.* Make a list of materials and supplies that tutors will have available and begin collecting them. If this if your first year of implementing a literacy tutoring program on your campus, you might divide your list into two columns—*essential* and *desirable*. Remember the principal's administrative assistant you invited to be on your volunteer literacy team? Available school funds and any *extra* supplies in the building are her expertise!

6. *Determine* where *the tutors will work with students.* Walk through the building and locate an area that will provide enough space for quiet and uninterrupted learning. Consistency matters. Reserve that space in your building for tutoring.

7. *Decide which grade levels and how many students you will be able to accommodate.* Visualizing the space and arrangements of tables in a

room or hallway you have chosen for tutoring sessions will help with this decision.

8. *Remember the three Cs: commitment, communication, and community!* These apply to your faculty and staff as well as your future volunteers. Schedule a time at a faculty meeting to explain the goals and expectations of your school's volunteer literacy tutoring program. Administer a survey (see a sample survey in Appendix A–5) to determine the willingness of teachers to become part of the literacy volunteer team. Ask teachers to complete the Helpful Information form and describe potential students who would benefit from individualized tutoring (see Appendix B–1).

9. *Establish a time line and designate responsibilities.* While the literacy coach or reading specialist will have the primary responsibility of supervising the volunteers during the year, members of the campus volunteer literacy team can help get things rolling. Decide who can help with recruiting volunteers, locating or ordering materials, setting up the tutoring space, or creating an attractive brochure to advertise your program. Choose dates for everything to be completed and write them on the calendar.

10. *Set up ways to communicate with the members of your team.* Schedule several follow-up meetings to discuss how things are going. Of course, technology is great; regular emails among the campus team keeps everyone informed and focused! Working together will help make your literacy volunteer program a success.

Now you are ready to recruit your volunteers. Don't worry! They are out there waiting to be found, you just have to know where to look. The word will spread quickly that you are looking for volunteers and the phone calls will start! Volunteers do not need to arrive with extensive training in literacy or even experience with students. You are looking for a few good men and women who have the energy and willingness to make a yearlong commitment, learn new skills and ways of working with students, and of course, who like to read and write themselves!

There are several ways to recruit literacy volunteers:

- Create a list of organizations and people you will contact and tell about your program. Consider retirement homes, churches, neighborhood associations, local businesses, or nearby community colleges.

■ Request time at these organizations' weekly or monthly meetings to make a short presentation about the need for volunteers and program you are implementing. The personal contact can make all the difference!

■ Prepare a simple attractive, one-page description of your volunteer program. An attractive brochure (see Appendix A–1) can be placed in your front office or distributed at local churches, neighborhood meetings, or interested businesses.

■ Ask a local church if you can talk to the congregation about how they can help your students. This is a good time to share pictures of your school and students (with permission). Don't forget to bring a sign-up sheet. You will be surprised how many people will sign up on the spot!

■ Make personal telephone calls to friends and to potential volunteers suggested by others.

■ Place a notice in the school newsletter.

■ Contact the public relations departments of businesses in your area. Many businesses expect their employees to volunteer at local schools.

■ Contact your local newspaper and ask to place a notice in the community section. You might ask them to write an article about your program.

■ Ask your own faculty and staff for suggestions. Many of them have family and friends who would be interested in tutoring.

To create a seamless program, it is imperative that the volunteers understand that this is a full-year commitment. Any wrinkles can be ironed out if your expectations are clear!

Roadmapping Your Program

The time available and the commitment you are willing to make to your literacy tutoring program will determine the model you adopt. This book focuses on two successful models that are currently being implemented in the Spring Branch Independent School District in Houston, Texas.

Model One—Hourly Tutoring Session Once a Week

Scheduling is less of an issue with this model. All the tutors come for the same hour each week. This model typically recruits volunteers who reside in a retirement home and are dependent on bus transportation. Basing your tutoring program on this model works well for schools that have time constraints and prefer supervised tutoring sessions. There are several advantages to this model.

1. Since the tutoring session occurs on the *same* day each week, the supervisor can be present and provide support during the sessions. Having the supervisor there to answer questions and concerns on the spot immediately clears up any misconceptions while adding to the knowledge base of the tutors.

2. By observing the interaction between the tutor and the student, the supervisor can also make notes and offer suggestions for the next session.

3. Time is usually available at the end of the hourly session for tutors and students to reflect, celebrate, and share with the whole group.

4. Additional time before and after the one-hour tutoring session allows for several things.

   ■ Before each session, tutors have time to read suggestions and responses from the classroom teacher.

   ■ After students leave the session, tutors have time to reflect on the lesson and send a message to the classroom teacher.

   ■ The supervisor can provide short, intensive mini-training sessions at the beginning or end of the hour.

5. Classroom teachers have time between tutoring sessions to determine the needs of the students and provide specific lessons to be completed. Placing a tutor tote in a central location provides a drop-off spot for teachers. The teachers use the portable tutor tote to drop off their weekly communication piece and new reading material. The supervisor simply carries this tote to the tutoring location.

Of course there are a few things to consider with this model. Since the supervisor is required to be present, this model works best with an assistant. The tutoring sessions can continue even if the supervisor is off campus. This colleague must be one who is willing to substitute when necessary. The time between tutoring sessions is also a factor. Meeting once a week does not allow tutors as much involvement with daily work with the student. The tutor is more dependent on the classroom teachers to provide the books and materials. It is critical that students involved in the tutoring program have teachers who support this model. While an hour-long session might allow for tutors to work with more than one student, tutors usually work with only one student thus limiting the number of students who might receive individualized instruction.

The following table is a brief description of the suggested components of the once-a-week model. A more detailed explanation of each tutoring component can be found in Chapter 4.

Once-a-Week Model

Time Component	Activities
The tutor shares, the student listens and enjoys. (5–10 minutes)	The first 5–10 minutes the tutor shares something from the world of print—a poem, a newspaper article, a favorite picture book, a chapter, or a photo album. This form of sharing models how reading is a part of our everyday lives. It's how we learn and how we're entertained. It keeps us thinking!
The student rereads a familiar book. (10 minutes)	The student practices fluent reading with expression. The tutor celebrates the student's reading.
The student reads new material. (15 minutes)	A new book on the student's instructional level is selected by the classroom teacher. Throughout the reading, they stop to think aloud, make connections, infer, and monitor meaning.
The student manipulates letters and works with words. (5 minutes)	Depending on the needs of the student, the tutor and the student manipulate letters, and build and sort words.
The student completes a writing activity. (10 minutes)	The student follows up with a reading response.
Sharing time. (5 minutes)	Volunteer/student pairs have an opportunity to share what they learned about themselves as readers.
Time for reflection. (5 minutes)	After students return to class, the tutors have time to write a short note to the teacher.

Model Two—Twice a Week with Flexible Hours

Model Two, while still providing structured tutoring sessions, allows for more flexibility on the part of the tutors. This model is best for tutors who have their own transportation and are willing to commit to at least two thirty-minute sessions a week. In this model, the tutoring sessions are planned around each tutor's schedule. During the initial training, tutors designate their days, times, and grade level preferences. (Tutors come on different days and times during the week.) The supervisor then checks classroom schedules and meets with teachers to determine the best day and time for students to be absent from the classroom. Based on this information, the tutors are matched with the appropriate students. This model also has several advantages.

1. Once the tutors are trained, the model tends to run itself. While the supervisor needs to check in periodically with the tutors, she does not need to be present during every session.

2. Tutors and students meet a least twice a week, which tends to provide more consistency to the instruction. Tutors can closely monitor the literacy development of their students, keeping track of books read, word work completed, and stories written.

3. Meeting twice a week provides continuity and more involvement with daily instruction. This means less interruption between discussions with intermediate-level students reading chapter books. During the writing portion of a session, tutors have time to help students with drafting, revising, and editing longer stories. Stories can be reread, revised, and published.

4. With this model, tutors often ask to tutor more than one student. Committing to working back-to-back with two students seems more practical to many tutors. (Note: An advantage for volunteers who commit to two students—student absences become less of a problem. Rarely are both students missing!) This means that more students can receive individualized instruction. Most tutors prefer to stay for an hour. Having half-hour sessions means less daily time out of the classroom for students. Many teachers prefer this arrangement.

5. After the initial sessions, the tutors become responsible for choosing books, planning for letter and word work, and determining any written responses to text. While the classroom teacher may occasionally send work with the student, the primary responsibility for the tutoring session falls on the tutor. Specific concerns about a student arising during the school year can be addressed by an occasional stop-and-chat by the supervisor. This provides an opportunity to share ideas or activities to support the student. Concerns and suggestions can also be communicated through a phone call or note attached to the student's folder or box (see Chapter 3).

As with model one, there are a few things to consider. Obviously, scheduling requires time and patience. Scheduling tutoring sessions around guided reading, music, health fitness, library time, lunch, and recess can be stressful. Supervisors will find it a challenge to create a plan that satisfies everyone's schedule. But just like anything else in life, good things take time. The payoff makes it all worthwhile. Here is a simple solution for scheduling (see also Appendix A–4 for an example).

- Write the days of the week across the top of a large piece of chart paper, starting with the second column.

- Down the lefthand side (first column), list times by the half hour. Make these boxes large enough to hold a sticky note.

- Write the names of each tutor and student on a sticky note. Use different colors to designate each grade level.

- Place each sticky note on the chart under the days and times that satisfy the schedule of both the classroom teacher and the tutor. A few rearrangements of these notes and the schedule starts to fall into place. Keeping this chart handy throughout the year provides a quick and accessible visual of the literacy tutoring program.

The success of this model depends on the flexibility of the tutor and classroom teacher. When teachers value tutors, and tutors feel empowered, rearranging a half-hour here or there for the benefit of a student is rarely a problem. This model requires more work early on, but once the schedule is in place, it runs very smoothly.

Because literacy volunteers are present throughout the week, the supervisor must build time into her schedule to periodically touch base with every tutor. Try some of the following ways to keep communication flowing between the supervisor and the tutor.

- Walk through the tutoring room once or twice a week and stop a moment to listen to a student read. Taking time to say, "Wow! That sounded just like the teacher!", or "How did you figure out that word?" will bring a smile to both the tutor's and the student's faces! Simply asking the tutor, "How is everything going?" often sparks a conversation about celebrations or concerns the tutor might have about a student.

- If there is a particular tutor you seem to miss on a regular basis, take the time to call her at home and find out how everything is going.

Model Two: Twice a Week with Flexible Hours

Time Component	Activities
Reading *to, with,* and *by* students. (10 minutes)	The tutor reads aloud *to* or *with* the student. Tutors share picture books, poetry, or newspaper articles. Students reread familiar books or chapters while tutors celebrate their success. Tutors introduce new material on the student's instructional level. Throughout the reading of the new text, the tutor and student *think aloud,* making connections, inferring, and monitoring meaning.
Letter and word work. (5 minutes)	Based on the student's needs the tutor and student manipulate magnetic letters, write words on erasable boards, or complete making words activities.
Writing *for, with,* and *by* students. (15 minutes)	The student responds in writing to a story, creates an alphabet book, or writes his own story.
Time for reflection!	After the student returns to class, the tutor reflects on the lesson, confers with or writes a note to the supervisor.

■ Create a mailbox accessible in the tutoring or supervisor's room where the supervisor or tutor (or the teacher) can communicate through written messages. Shoe bags with multiple pouches labeled with each tutor's name make great mailboxes! Appendix C has examples of simple communication forms.

Because tutoring occurs throughout the day and week, student absences, unscheduled assemblies, or even a field trip that didn't make it on the calendar can be an issue with this model. The supervisor and the classroom teacher must come up with a way of notifying the tutor when a student will be absent (see Chapter 5).

The preceding table is a brief description of a tutoring program involving multiple weekly sessions. A more detailed explanation of tutoring components can be found in Chapter 4.

Regardless of the model you choose, in order to be successful there are several nonnegotiable factors to consider.

1. Students should be taken out of class during language arts rather than math, science, or social studies.

2. Tutoring should provide *supplemental* reading and writing instruction, not replace it. Consistent days and times are agreed upon before tutoring begins so that students do not miss small-group instruction in reading and writing.

3. Flexibility is required on the tutor's part as there will be times throughout the year when classroom work may be the focus of the tutoring session.

4. Teachers are responsible for identifying their students who would benefit from tutoring (see Appendix B–1).

5. No *double dipping*. It must be understood that students who are receiving other services such as special education, ESL, literacy intervention, or reading recovery are not candidates for tutoring.

6. Communication between the tutor and the teacher must take place before or after each session (see Appendix C–2).

7. Collaboration between supervisor, teacher, and tutor is essential.

8. All volunteers are screened according to district policy.

9. Confidentiality issues are addressed in the initial training.

10. Commitment, communication, and community are necessary for success!

Both models are very effective. As the supervisor of the volunteer literacy tutoring program, which one you choose to implement will depend entirely on your needs and time commitment.

CHAPTER 3

Kit and Kaboodle

Once you determine a literacy tutoring model that meets your needs, it is time to start gathering *tools* and materials for the tutors. From pencils to magnetic letters, journals to books, meeting the needs of each student will make the tutoring experience successful and rewarding. In a learner-centered environment, students work side by side with a more knowledgeable tutor as they explore together the world of written text. Close observation by well-trained tutors provides many opportunities for teachable moments. Being able to quickly grab magnetic letters, an erasable board, or just the right book will make these teachable moments come alive.

Tutoring Kits

Access to a literacy toolkit helps to create a smooth and successful tutoring experience. Having markers, scissors, glue, and other materials in one container means more time reading and writing, and less time gathering and searching. Everything is right at the tutor's fingertips. A simple, medium-sized plastic basket found at any discount store is an easy way to store materials (see pictures on pages 13 and 14). There should be enough tutoring kits for *each* tutor and student. Tutors pick up a tutoring kit, take it to the tutoring area, and are ready to go!

Medium-sized baskets allow plenty of room for a variety of literacy materials. Markers, pens, and pencils ensure that writing materials are

always on hand. Small erasable boards and erasers (old socks or tissues) fit perfectly in these baskets, too. Magnetic erasable boards have a double purpose—the student can manipulate magnetic letters and practice fluent writing with letters and words. You can find these erasable boards at most teacher supply stores. Magnetic oven covers come in different sizes, shapes, and colors and can be used as erasable boards. They fit perfectly in the basket. Don't forget to check out your local hardware store. They usually carry large sheets of *shower board* that is very similar to the material used for dry erase boards. Tell them what you need it for, and they are usually quite willing to cut it into the size you need.

That basket isn't full yet! Include cover-up tape or correction tape. Especially for younger students, having correction tape says, "It's okay. Go ahead and try. Write what you think it sounds like and looks like. We can fix it later!" Younger students may also have difficulty with spacing between words. Fingers work well, but consider getting some tongue depressors from the nurse to use as spacers. Draw a face at the top and you have a *Space Man*! (Tutors, teachers, and students seem to like the idea of "Space Man.")

Keep the baskets filled with different colors and sizes of sticky notes, with and without lines. Handing students a sticky note encourages them to write down those tricky or interesting words. Or, tutors can stop and ask, "What's that voice in your head saying right now? Let's make a note of your thinking." A sticky note provides just enough space to write a question, a personal connection, or a prediction.

Emphasize the reading–writing connection by including a resealable bag full of blank minibooks. Stationery as well as teacher supply stores sell notepads in a variety of shapes and sizes. Tear off one sheet of the shaped notepad, and using five or six blank sheets of paper, trace around the shape, staple, and you have a ready-made book in the shape of dog, cat, or pumpkin. Students can use these books for writing exercises like retelling; summarizing the beginning, middle, and end of a story; or even writing the *next* chapter of the book they just read. Encourage younger students to write their own story by adding a variety of stickers to your resealable bag. Since stickers are often packaged according to a theme, they can serve as a springboard for creating a new story. Include single sheets of the individual notepad designs for more advanced readers and writers. Students love to use these to write character descriptions, memory snapshots, and book recommendations or reviews.

It is key that tutoring tools are *easy* and *accessible*. Of course, the availability of materials will depend on your budget and space. Here is a quick checklist of materials that can easily become part of a tutor's toolkit.

- pens
- pencils
- markers
- crayons
- scissors
- glue sticks

- spacers
- sticky notes
- correction tape
- highlighter tape
- blank minibooks for writing
- highlighter

Book, Books, Books

A successful tutoring program requires books that meet the students' needs. Access to books representing different readability levels, genres, and interests builds the foundation for building successful readers. Tutors need access to two types of books: (1) books that can be read *to* the student, and (2) books that can be read *with* and *by* students.

Books for Read-Aloud—Reading *to* the Student

Near the tutoring baskets, create a minilibrary of read-aloud books. Start off by asking for donations from teachers and parents. Books from your school and the public library also make great additions. Most public libraries allow teachers to check out books for up to six weeks.

Once you have a selection of read-aloud books, sort and label them according to several categories. A rule of thumb: The more variety the tutors have to choose from, the more likely they will choose books that meet the students' needs and interests. For younger students, baskets of alphabet, nursery rhymes, or predictable and patterned books will make it easier for tutors to grab the right book. Additional baskets might be divided into picture books (fiction and nonfiction). Sort nonfiction books into biographies or science and social studies topics. Easy-to-read chapter and more complex chapter books should also be part of your library. Check with a librarian about old copies of children's magazines that can be added to the read-aloud library. Poetry appeals to all ages, so don't forget to include a poetry basket! Decorating a basket of seasonal or holiday books also makes a great addition to your minilibrary. Display *new* books on occasion. These may be books that the students haven't seen before, but will keep your minilibrary fresh and interesting. One word of caution: Stamp or write "literacy tutors" on the books in your minilibrary. Labeling your books will help guard against loss. Regardless of the size of your minilibrary, providing read-aloud selections for your tutors will help make the tutoring experience run more smoothly. (See Appendix F–2 for suggested read-aloud books.)

Books to Read *with* and *by* the Students

Tutors need access to books on the student's instructional and independent reading level. If your school has chosen a tutoring model where the classroom teacher is responsible for matching a book with the student, this area becomes less of a concern. The teacher will send an appropriate book with the student. But if you expect the tutor to be responsible (after the initial sessions) for finding the right book, then you will need to provide a *leveled* library.

If your school has a guided reading book room, the tutors should have access. This means at your initial training sessions (see Chapter 4), tutors need instruction in two areas: (1) what is meant by *levels*; and (2) how to check out books. Close proximity to the guided reading book room also means quick access for the tutors. So consider the distance between your guided book room and the chosen tutoring area.

Depending on the size and scope of your tutoring program, you may decide to build a library of leveled books to be kept in the tutoring area. Creating a separate set of leveled books takes time and some ingenuity, but there are several advantages:

1. Tutors do not need to be trained how to use the guided book room.

2. Guided reading book sets do not have to be *shared* between tutors and classroom teachers.

3. Your leveled library can reside in the tutoring room.

While responsibility for book selection falls on the supervisor at the beginning, tutors will soon be knowledgeable enough to choose books on their own. By having baskets of leveled books readily available, it shows tutors you have confidence in their ability to match a book to their student.

Now, you might be asking: (1) Where do I find books for a literacy tutor leveled library? and (2) Where am I going to get money for the books and tutoring kits? For leveled books, consult catalogues from reliable companies such as Rigby, Wright Group, Heinemann, or National Geographic (see page 109). Leveled trade books can be used for tutoring developing and transitional readers. There are other excellent resources to help you choose leveled books from your school or public library (see Pinnell and Fountas 1996). You will want a variety of books at a number of different levels. Consult Appendix F–3 for reading level comparison chart.

Locating funds for books and materials is always a concern. If you are resourceful and persistent, however, you'll find the money. Check with your administrator, parent–teacher association, or local church group about any available funds. Talk with area businesses or major chain stores. Many of them have funds set aside for school programs. Grants are another source of money. Local, state, and federal agencies offer grants that can be used for tutoring programs.

If you do have a guided reading book room, there are often sets of books that have been narrowed down to one or two books and need to be pulled from the shelf. Add these incomplete sets to begin building a leveled set of books for the tutors. Don't forget to check with your librarian. She often has discarded books that she would be willing to donate. You can also let parents or school staff know that you'd accept gently used books. You will be surprised how many books find their way to your tutoring library. There are lots of books out there; your job is to locate and catalogue them for easy access. Whether you are thinking about read-aloud or leveled books, never say no to a free book!

A Space for Everything and Everything in Its Space

Finding a location for the tutors and the students to work is always a concern. Ideally, the tutoring should take place in a quiet room reserved for only tutors and students. If you are lucky enough to have an extra room, place the books, tutoring kits, and other materials and supplies in this room. Be thoughtful about spacing tables and chairs around the room to provide enough quiet space for simultaneous tutoring sessions. If the room is large enough, several tutoring sessions can be going on concurrently.

No unoccupied rooms in the building? Then finding a quiet space for tutors and their students will require a little more creativity. Using partitions to set up tutoring booths in an open area or hallway is one solution. Check with the librarian to see if you can use part of the library. You might be able to move desks into the hallway, although classes walking by can be a distraction. Some specialists in the building might be willing to let you use part of their rooms when they do not have classes. Where there's a will, there's a way!

Once you've decided where the tutors will work with their students, create a space where all books and materials are readily available. This space does not need to be large. Inexpensive bookshelves, an empty cupboard, or even a cart on wheels can provide a central place to store materials. You will need enough space for some of the following items.

Tutoring Kits
Read-Aloud Mini-library
Leveled Books
Individual Magazine Boxes
or Tutoring Tote with Individual Files

Grades K–2	Grades 3–5
• magnetic letters in sorting tray	• tagboard letters in sorting tray
• ABC or sight word bingo	• word games
• modeling clay	• spiral notebooks
• alphabet charts and puzzles	• dictionaries
	• maps
	• response/reflection journals

A Box of Their Own

Each student should have his own box or file folder labeled with his name and his tutor's name. These individual boxes or files can hold the student's familiar books, response journal, or stories they are writing. They also give the supervisor a logical place to put interview and assessment forms, new books, or notes from you or the teacher. Individual student boxes or files make it easy for you to monitor the student's progress. Having everything organized in a central place saves the tutor time and energy. Tutors will appreciate arriving and finding all their materials organized and accessible. A quick weekly check by the supervisor is usually enough to ensure that all materials, books, and student boxes and files are in order. The more organized the materials and supplies, the more smoothly the tutoring program will run!

CHAPTER 4

Training Tutors 1, 2, 3!

Volunteer literacy tutors will need training and support in order to provide effective instruction, but the limited time available to supervisors and tutors alike often necessitates *compacting* information. While there are many training models, this chapter focuses on a two-day training model. It is important not to overwhelm your new tutors, so scheduling two half-days of training often works best. The following goals will set the tone for the first day.

1. Share the research behind one-to-one tutoring.

2. Explain the benefits of tutoring students.

3. Clarify the expectations and components of a typical tutoring session.

4. Give an explanation of the reading process.

5. Demonstrate specific activities for a successful tutoring session.

Day 1

While the schedule will vary, the following is an overview of how the first day might look.

1. *Welcome the tutors to your school.* Introduce yourself and any staff members present. Invite your school administrators to attend your first session. Their presence will support the philosophy that literacy tutors

play a critical role in your school's literacy program. Have the tutors introduce themselves, giving a brief explanation of who they are and why they decided to tutor.

2. *Start with an inspirational read-aloud.* *Mrs. Spitzer's Garden* by Edith Pattou is a great read-aloud book to break the ice with the tutors. Hand the tutors a package of seeds as a symbol of the "flowers" they will help to grow. (Check Appendix F–1 for suggestions for other books to read aloud to tutors.)

3. *Share the following quotation.* Consider the following quote from Pinnell and Fountas (1997), "Literacy volunteers can give children special attention that invites them into the world of books, and written language and helps them realize what an important part reading and writing will play in their lives" (x). Let the tutors know how you appreciate their willingness to participate in your school's tutoring program. Maintaining your successful tutoring program depends in part on your ability to make the tutors feel like an integral part of students' literacy development.

4. *Briefly review the expectations of your tutoring program.* No matter if your tutors will be tutoring once, twice, or three times a week, this initial review lets them know the kind of commitment you expect.

5. *Discuss current research related to tutoring (see Introduction).* Research consistently shows the effectiveness of working one-to-one with a student (Wasik 1998; Cohen, Kulik, and Kulik 1982; Juel 1996). Letting tutors know your program is based on research demonstrates your commitment to creating an effective and sound program for your school.

6. *Talk with the tutors about tutoring tips* (see Chapter 1 from the companion book *You Said Yes!*). This chapter from the companion book allows the tutor to sample the items from the tutoring session menu. It reads like a preview of coming events. Without overwhelming them, these tutoring tips give the tutor enough information about the reading and writing process to help them feel empowered and willing to commit to a student's literacy development.

7. A successful literacy tutoring program demands that tutors understand what reading is all about. Chapter 2 in the companion book, *You Said Yes!,* "Reading: It's Okay to Make Mistakes," provides basic information about the reading process. Remember, most tutors are not

reading teachers. Inexperienced tutors, like many noneducators, believe teaching phonics is synonymous with teaching reading. Words like *semantic* (makes sense), *syntactic* (sounds right), or *graphophonemic* (looks right) are not part of tutors' vocabulary (see Appendix E–2). Viewing reading as a meaning-making process is new territory for them. Most adults believe either telling a student every unknown word or saying "sound it out" is the best way to help a student learn. You will need to gently nudge them toward a new understanding of the reading process. Show them how phonics is necessary, but it is only one component of reading. Students need to have a toolbox of strategies to pull from when faced with unknown words. Explain how *prompting* will help students pull out the best tool to support their reading. Some prompts to consider follow.

- "Think of a word that looks the same."
- "Start over!"
- "Say the first sound."
- "Try it. Skip. Read on. Go back!"
- "Look at the picture."
- "What would make sense?"
- "Sound it out."

Supporting students' reading is like the proverb—If you give a man a fish, he'll eat one meal. If you teach a man to fish, he'll eat for a lifetime. One goal of tutoring—creating lifetime readers!

8. Once tutors have a basic understanding of the reading process, take time to demonstrate what is meant by fluent reading. Chapter 3, "Read It Like the Teacher!" from the companion book *You Said Yes!*, focuses on the issue of fluency. You might be asking, What is so important about fluency? Tutors often view fluency simply as accurate decoding. According to Griffith and Rasinski (2004), reading requires the ability to decode and comprehend the text. Fluent reading demands more than reading every word correctly. Meaning is also carried through the intonation, pitch, expression, and phrasing of the reading (Rasinski 2003). Once the tutors have a deeper understanding of fluency, it is time for *active* participation. Have the tutors participate in a choral or echo reading of a short poem (see Appendix G–1

and G–2 for samples of poems to use). A short demonstration of how Reader's Theater works is another way to demonstrate a way to focus on fluency. Check out the following websites for Reader's Theatre scripts: *www.readerstheatre.com* and *www.readinglady.com*.

9. Take some time to explain what the tutoring sessions will involve. (See Chapter 2 from *You Said Yes!* for a more detailed explanation of two literacy tutoring models.) Be sure the tutors understand that the suggested minutes in this book for each component are only guidelines. The time spent on each component will depend on which tutoring model you choose as well as the student's strengths and needs. While the models have different time constraints, the basic components are the same. Since this is the first day, focus on explaining how the tutoring session will include reading *to*, *with*, and *by* students.

   ■ Discuss reading *to*, *with*, and *by* students. Remember that showing is better than telling. Model reading and thinking aloud with a picture book from the tutoring minilibrary. Use a big book like *Mrs. Wishy-Washy* by Joy Cowley or a poem to demonstrate shared reading or reading *with* students (see Appendix G–1 and G–2 for examples of short poems). Provide tutors with hands-on experience with leveled books by letting them go through the baskets filled with books from simple, one-line-per-page picture books to chapter books. Give them an opportunity to look through the different levels. Point out changes in print size, supportive illustrations, and text complexity. Demonstrate book introductions, or book walks, and give tutors opportunities to practice with each other. Review the idea of *prompts*. Refer to the Venn diagram in Appendix E–2. Share examples of laminated bookmarks with a few key prompts (see Appendix E–5). Explain how these prompts will be available along with other tutoring materials.

About now your tutors will probably be silently screaming, "Too much information!" Send them off with their package of seeds and assure them that everything takes time to grow, including knowledge! Before they leave, give each tutor two sticky notes. Ask them to write one thing they learned on a sheet of bulletin board paper labeled "Green Sprout!" (new learning) and "Still a Seed!" (questions).

Day 2

If possible, the second session should take place the next day. You don't want too many days falling between sessions. Tutors will have many questions following the first session that need to be answered as quickly as possible. Greet your tutors and welcome them back to the second session. Don't worry! They will return! Acknowledge their uncertainty about becoming a literacy tutor. They are probably feeling a little overwhelmed. Tell them how even experienced teachers feel overwhelmed after a workshop. No one expects them to remember everything. Just like anything new—with time and practice—knowledge and confidence grow. They will be supporting the students, but you will be available to support them.

The following goals will allow for review while providing some new information.

1. Review the reading process.

2. Understand what a proficient reader does before, during, and after reading.

3. Explain how to write *for* and *with* students and how to encourage independent writing.

4. Consider the role of phonics in reading and writing.

5. Clarify the components of the tutoring session.

6. Take a tour of the building and explain the orientation packet.

Here's how Day Two might go.

1. Start with a short, humorous read-aloud. For example, *My Rotten Red-Headed Older Brother*, by Patricia Polacco is a story that both children and adults enjoy. During this time, review the concept of *read-aloud* or reading *to* students. Explain to the tutors how you will be thinking aloud as you read. Tutors will find a list of ideas for thinking aloud in Chapters 6 and 7 in the companion book *You Said Yes!* Never pass up an opportunity to model!

2. Check the "Green Sprout" (new learning) and "Still a Seed" (questions) board from the first session. Take time to answer all their questions.

3. Quickly review the information about the reading process from the first session. Use the Venn Diagram (Appendix E–2) to go over the cueing systems: *semantic* (makes sense), *syntactic* (sounds right), and *graphophonemic* (looks right). It is important to clear up any misconceptions early. If the tutors understand from the beginning that reading is a meaning-making process, they are less likely to focus solely on the phonics component.

4. Keep in mind that most volunteers are very concerned about phonics. It is still a hot topic with educators and noneducators alike and is likely to be addressed throughout the tutoring session. Assure the tutors that phonics *is* important especially for beginning readers, however, the key point to make is that letter and word work will be *embedded* in authentic reading and writing activities. Demonstrate some simple activities with magnetic letters. The following are a few suggestions for giving tutors some hands-on experience.

   Explain how they might:

   ■ place magnetic letters in alphabetical order at the top of the table or large piece of paper

   ■ have students *pull-down* letters and build their names or names of friends

   ■ ask students to match upper- and lowercase letters

   ■ tell students to build known words like *the*, *and*, *to*, or *is*

   ■ have students manipulate letters to build new words like *at* to *it* to *hit* to *hat*

Use tagboard alphabet letters to demonstrate how developing and transitional readers are still continuing to learn about words. A wide variety of books are available with ideas for making words (see Appendx E–10, page 88 for an example). Or, create your own activity. Give tutors the letters that spell the word *literacy*. Have them make as many words as they can from those letters. You might also ask them to make specific words like *it, at, rat, cat, ace, ate, race, trace, crate,* and so on. Tell them to change one letter at a time to create a new word. The tutors enjoy these activities and they quickly see how word study is valuable for students at each grade level. Your live tutoring demonstration (discussed later) will provide an excellent opportunity to

show tutors that letter and word work will be an integral part of the tutoring session. They will be able to observe how this component of the session can be integrated into authentic reading and writing.

5. This is a good time to discuss the reading–writing connection with the tutors (see chapter 4, "Reading and Writing Go Hand in Hand," in the companion book *You Said Yes!*). Show them examples of simple dictated stories, summaries, character webs, or personal narratives. You might read aloud a book like *The Relatives Came* by Cynthia Rylant. Ask the tutors to write a short descriptive paragraph about one of their favorite relatives. Give them time to share their stories. The chap-

ter, "So Much to Do! So Little Time!" in the companion book *You Said Yes!* provides great ideas to help tutors see the connection between reading *to, with,* and *by* students and writing. It is important to take time to explain the difference between writing *for* and *with* students and expecting students to write independently. The concept of inter-active writing or sharing the pen will probably be new to most tutors. If possible, invite a student in and demonstrate how to make a take-home book.

6. So what about spelling? Tutors are often unsure about how to handle spelling. Explain to them how spelling helps the reader follow what the writer is saying. When writing with children, the goal should be to help the student get better at her spelling. Demonstrate how to use Elkonin Boxes (see Appendix E–8, page 86) or Marie Clay's Have a Go strategy in Appendix E–9, Give It a Try, page 87.

7. Tutors need to see an *authentic* tutoring session. A live tutoring ses-sion is the best way for tutors to observe what might happen during a thirty-minute session. Ask a student you know well to role play as a student during a tutoring session. Model the critical components of a typical tutoring session. The great thing about a live demonstration is you can stop and discuss what is happening. Tutors can also ask questions about everything and anything. The next best thing to a live demonstration is showing a video of a tutoring session. Creating a tu-toring video doesn't require a professional cameraman. If you have a reading recovery teacher on campus, you might ask to videotape a ses-sion. Or, videotape yourself conducting a tutoring session.

8. At this point, take time to carefully explain what good readers do (Chapters 6 and 7) in the companion book *You Said Yes!* After reading these motivating and easy-to-read chapters, tutors will walk away be-lieving they *can* make a difference in a student's literacy development. Confidence will continue to develop as tutors begin to take on specific activities that support the needs of individual students.

9. By this point, your tutors have enough information to send them off with students. Assure them that you will take them to meet their stu-dent the first day and help them get started. Explain the get-acquainted interview and interest forms (see Appendix A–9, page 57 and E–12–E–14, pages 91–96). Take a few minutes to describe the initial ses-sions with a student. Hand the tutors a list of ideas to help them get started on the right foot.

The Initial Tutoring Session

- Go through introductions of tutor, student, and classroom teacher by supervisor.

- Complete a get-acquainted interview and interest forms.

- Share a picture album with your student.

- Enjoy a read-aloud together.

- Give the student a choice of books and ask them to read to you.

- Ask the student to tell you about the book the teacher sent.

- Play a game like alphabet bingo, "Go Fish" using sight words, or word board games.

Finish this second day of training by taking a tour of the building. Start with the tutoring area so tutors see the materials and supplies available for them. Introduce the tutors to the librarian, the nurse, the administrative assistant, and any other key office personal who will be involved with the tutors. Make sure tutors know the procedure for fire drills and where they should take students if a fire drill occurs while they are with a student.

Don't forget to give each tutor an orientation packet with your phone number, email address, their student's teacher and classrooms, and school calendar (see Appendix A–10 for additional ideas). Before the tutors leave, if you have chosen the more flexible hours model, have them sign up for the days and times they prefer to tutor. Explain that it will take a few days for you to pair them up with a student, but you will be calling them soon. Again thank the tutors for their gift of time and reassure them that you will always be available to support them as literacy tutors.

Tutors will need ongoing training throughout the year. There are several ways to add to the knowledge base of your tutors: (1) schedule short one-hour follow-up sessions throughout the year; (2) send out an *idea* newsletter; (3) hold brief individual conferences before or after tutoring sessions; or (4) create a "Note to the Tutor" sheet to fill out and give to the tutor (see Appendix C–1). In addition to the two-day initial session, follow-up sessions, conversations, and notes will continue to empower your tutors without overwhelming them. They will want to keep coming back for more.

CHAPTER 5

There's Trouble Ahead

As with any program, there are always a few potential snags. When coordinating a literacy volunteer program, be proactive! Try to anticipate any problems and have a system in place to deal with them. The following ideas might head off any future storms and keep the skies clear and sunny.

Absenteeism

▪ It is *very important* to let tutors know when a student is absent. Tutors must feel you value and appreciate their time. Create a communication system between you and the classroom teacher to check attendance every morning. For instance, the teacher could notify the supervisor with the name of the absent student. Many tutors have email, which could also be used to let them know when a student is absent. Of course, classroom teachers are very busy. Taping a small, colorful card on the desk with the days and times of the student's tutoring sessions printed on the card provides a visual reminder when a student is absent (see Appendix B–4). The teacher can quickly check to see if the student has a tutor coming that day and notify the supervisor.

▪ There may be times when *you* are absent. Post a chart in a conspicuous place with the names and phone numbers of the tutors, the student(s) they tutor, along with the days and times of tutoring sessions. Then make sure you have arranged for someone else to call tutors if a student is absent.

■ Give tutors a copy of the district and your school's monthly calendar to inform them of holidays, inservice days, special school programs, and field trips. Occasionally, though, field trips or school programs do not make it to the calendar. You may need to call several tutors or, if possible, a volunteer liaison could help you inform tutors. Enlist the help of grade level team leaders to notify you of any last-minute changes in the schedule.

■ Even though the tutors have a copy of the district and school calendar, it is always a good idea to remind them with a note or phone call of upcoming events. Post brightly colored notes on the tutoring room door or in student boxes to announce dates that might interfere with tutoring.

■ Occasionally a student is not in his classroom because of unavoidable changes in a teacher's schedule. It is helpful if the teacher has a message board on the outside of her door explaining where the class is at a particular time of day. This avoids a search of the building.

Tutoring Problems

Volunteers, especially inexperienced ones, will occasionally have problems with either managing the tutoring session or a student's behavior. Observing tutoring sessions will provide you with the information you need to provide support for the tutor. It is also important to have a communication system in place so that tutors can convey any concerns they might have. A volunteer may become discouraged and appeal to you for help, or the volunteer may not realize there are problems. The following are some ideas that may help.

Difficulty Managing the Task

■ It is best for you, the supervisor, to work with the tutor individually when the tutor runs into problems. Taking the time to demonstrate a task with a student while the tutor watches can be very powerful. You might say, "Would you mind if I show you something I learned that might be helpful?"

■ *Always* praise and encourage the tutor and explain that it is not easy to accomplish all the tasks required to support a student's reading. Explain that with time, everything will get easier.

Difficulty Managing a Student's Behavior

■ Model some ways to work with the student: (1) giving explicit directions; (2) being pleasant but firm; (3) moving the student to a different location, to avoid distractions; (4) changing the activities and pace of the lesson.

■ Ask the classroom teacher for advice on ways of working with the specific student.

■ Help the volunteer understand how to make the session more engaging or interesting for the student. Explain that students have different learning styles and may need to approach the task in a different manner. The situation may improve by simply introducing a new game or different writing material. (For example, one student refused to write until the tutor sent home a disposable camera and asked him to take pictures of himself with his friends and family. The student couldn't wait to write about his pictures!)

■ Talk with the student and the classroom teacher together in order to determine what might be causing the behavior. Explain to the student how his behavior is interfering with his learning. Help the student understand that having an individual tutor is a privilege and that if his behavior doesn't improve, the tutor will be assigned another student.

■ If all else fails, you may need to assign the tutor another student. Make it clear to the tutor that this happens occasionally and in no way is a reflection of their instruction. The student simply needs a different kind of support. Help the tutor understand that the student's behavior is beyond their control and some simply need a professional expert. Having to reassign a student does not happen very often especially if your initial matching of tutor and student was done thoughtfully and carefully.

CHAPTER 6

So . . . Do I Really Want to Do This?

Volunteers need to feel that their time and efforts are appreciated. A common complaint of volunteers is feeling unappreciated. You will gain a lot of mileage if you recognize your tutors. They will return year after year! Part of your role as the tutoring supervisor means providing ongoing support and encouragement. The following suggestions lay the foundation for maintaining an effective tutoring program.

Welcoming Your Volunteer Literacy Tutors

■ Make special name tags for the tutors. Name tags that say *Literacy Tutor* or *Literacy Volunteer* validate their role in your school's literacy program.

■ Create a welcoming bulletin board including the tutors' pictures and names.

■ Host a get-acquainted breakfast for tutors and students. Read aloud the book *Wilfrid Gordon McDonald Partridge* by Mem Fox to the tutors and students before they meet for breakfast. You could also read this book to the tutors during the initial training sessions. Meet with the students who will be part of the tutoring program a few days before the get-acquainted breakfast. Explain how they have been assigned a special friend who will be talking and reading with them. Read *Wilfred Gordon McDonald Partridge* and show them examples of artifacts. Tutors and students can then bring one artifact to the get-acquainted breakfast to share. The artifact might be something from long ago, something that makes them laugh or cry, or something precious as gold. This item will serve as a catalyst for conversation.

■ Include a section in your school newsletter explaining the literacy tutoring program and welcoming the tutors to your school. Make sure the tutors receive copies of the newsletter!

■ Sending a letter home introducing the tutor is a great way to start building communication between the tutor, student, and parents. (See sample letter in Appendix A–7, page 55.)

The First Days

■ Regardless of the model you implement, it is important that you are available when the tutors arrive for their first tutoring session. Tutors and students may be a little nervous on the first day and a personal introduction will help smooth the way.

■ Closely supervise the first few sessions to ensure everything is going well. A simple, "How is everything going?" will help lower the stress level of your new tutors.

Building the Relationship

It is critical to cement the relationship between the student, tutor, supervisor, and school community.

■ Monthly surprises will always bring a smile to your tutors' faces! Set out a bowl of candies with a note, *"Kisses and wishes for a great day!"* Fill a basket full of student-created bookmarks, pictures, or poems for tutors to take home. Decorate the tutoring room with balloons and banners created by students. The list is endless. Remember you don't need to spend a lot of money or time—a little support will go a long way!

■ Periodically write notes to the tutors thanking them for their time and caring attitude toward the students. Slip these notes into the tutors' mailboxes or send through regular mail.

■ The relationship between the tutor and the student is very important. You might have postcards available for the tutor to send to the student on their birthday or holiday. Or, the student might send a letter or postcard to the tutor.

▦ Serving refreshments for the tutors and students on special holidays is another way of showing your appreciation. You might provide the student with a small gift for the tutor such as a bookmark, pen, or gift certificate to a bookstore. Local craft stores have wooden cut-outs with holiday themes. These can be quickly painted. Add a magnet to the back to create a special gift. Place the magnet and a holiday poem in a plastic bag. (See Appendix D–7, page 75, for an example of "Valentine Thoughts.")

▦ Many schools have a volunteer luncheon or breakfast for all the volunteers in the school. A nice touch is to have an end-of-the-year brunch just for the literacy tutors and their students (see Appendix D–3, page 70). The tutors are especially appreciative of a photograph, a picture, a letter, or a note from their student.

▦ At the end of the year, don't forget to write a letter to each volunteer thanking them for their support and hard work!

Supervising a volunteer literacy tutoring program takes time and commitment. Yet for some students, the individualized instruction that one-to-one tutoring provides is exactly what they need to launch them on the wonderful adventure of being literate individuals. At the end of our first year of implementing a literacy tutoring program, we asked the students to respond to this question: "If another student said, 'I wish I had a tutor!' what would you say to them?" One young student answered, "Well I will tell them that you can't because you read well and spell gooder than me. I just need help."

There are times when tutors may even ask themselves if they are making a difference. Reassure them by repeating the question that is always asked by students when a tutor must miss a tutoring session, "Where is my reading teacher?" Even though students may have difficulty expressing their appreciation for the time a volunteer tutor spends with them, they always notice when the tutor isn't there. For some students, the social side of individualized instruction is just as critical as the academic.

If you already have a volunteer literacy tutoring program in place, that's great! We hope the information in this book provides you with the resources needed to make your program even better. For those of you who do not have a literacy tutoring program in place, consider initiating one. Just look around; plenty of people are out there who want to help our students and our schools. They're just waiting to be asked. *Communicate* with your *community* of potential volunteers and the *commitment* will follow. Start small and the word will spread! Then you can stand back and watch the seeds you've sown turn into a most amazing and bountiful harvest.

CHAPTER 7

Reflections of a Supervisor

We've always had volunteers at Sherwood who were quite willing to read with our children, but we saw a need to train adult volunteers to work one-on-one with our students who are at risk for reading failure, to arm them to be independent readers and writers.

—Patricia Oliver
Journal Entry
May, 1999

I remember saying the above words during an interview with a reporter from a local newspaper. But as I read the article, I began to think about what the reporter failed to say. Yes, we did have a need for volunteers who understood the intricacies of the reading process. Yes, we had noticed that some of our students were receiving information from the tutor that conflicted with what they had heard in the classroom. Yes, some of our students faced a daily struggle with letters, sounds, and words every time they picked up a book. And yes, classroom teachers didn't always have the time to give as much individualized instruction as they would have liked. Yet what the reporter left out was the "human" side of our volunteer literacy tutoring program.

I remember sitting in the library the first time we met to discuss the possibility of establishing a volunteer literacy tutoring program on our campus. My administrator and I had already talked about the kind of program we wanted. We already had a volunteer program of sorts in the building—volunteers were assigned to a teacher and would spend an hour reading for a few minutes with every child. But we also noticed well-meaning tutors holding the books in their own laps, pointing to the words, turning the pages, covering up the pictures, and immediately supplying any unknown words. The student rarely did any reading "work" on their own. Since we wanted an effective research-based program that truly met the needs of our students, we knew there might be some resistance from teachers and potential volunteers.

But during our first meeting with our campus volunteer team, I found myself surrounded by teachers and volunteers who may have been a little unsure at first, but who were willing look into revamping our volunteer literacy tutoring program. Their willingness to change and move forward was based on one critical fact—let whatever is best for the students guide your thinking and planning.

After showing them the research about what makes an effective tutoring program, we began brainstorming how we would find the volunteers. Tom Potts, who represented our Pines Presbyterian Church partner, was somewhat skeptical about how many people would be willing to commit to two days a week, but he agreed to spread the word. As he left the meeting, even he wasn't sure if he wanted to be a literacy tutor. What still amazes me today—Tom Potts and his wife Barbara were the first two people to sign up!

We announced our program expectations, including a two-day mandatory initial training session, through several means: (1) a trifold poster explaining our program displayed at Pines Presbyterian Church; (2) notices in the area and school newspaper; and (3) brochures left in the front office of our school. Volunteers literally began flocking to the building. I was hopeful we would have ten volunteers the first year; we had twenty! I was truly overwhelmed by the number of people who were willing to give up two mornings or afternoons a week to work with one, two, and sometimes three students.

The first day of training, I was nervous. Who were these individuals sitting in front of me? Would they be able to understand the complexities of reading and what we expected of them as literacy tutors? But after the introductions were over, I wasn't worried. I met retired teachers, company managers, and executives. I met mothers and dads, some with empty nests and some with children still at home. I met a practicing lawyer, a nurse, and employees of a local business. They all had one thing in common—the desire to make a change in the life of a student's literacy development. I was surrounded by people who were filled with a wealth of background knowledge and information!

All these wonderful, knowledgeable, and eager individuals sat for two days and learned about the complexities of reading, the different levels of books, and how to "prompt" students as they read. They practiced with manipulating magnetic and tagboard letters. They wrote on erasable boards. They cut and pasted to make alphabet and minibooks. They took notes and asked questions as they watched a teacher and student interact in a tutoring situation. And at the end of two days, they actually still wanted to be a volunteer literacy tutor!

The tutors eventually met their student (or students), spent time getting to know each other, and the rest of year went smoothly. Okay, there were a few bumps and ruts in the road. Student absences were a problem. Students were in the library, in the computer room, or at recess when they should have been in their own rooms. Students moved or were placed in different programs and the tutor had to be reassigned another student. Occasionally I would find myself distracted with all the other hats I wore throughout the day and fail to monitor as well as I should. We both learned—the tutors and me.

Were we successful the first year? Yes, the students made substantial academic progress. But the success of our volunteer literacy program was demonstrated by the concern of our tutors. Tutors continually asked, "How are they doing in the classroom?" "How did they do on that test?" "Is there anything else I should be doing?" Success also showed in the faces, actions, and voices of our students. I saw success when a young student jumped up from his seat, knocking over his chair as he ran to his tutor, smiling and saying, "Where were you last week? I missed you." I saw success as the tutor and student walked away, heads together, whispering about yesterday, today, and tomorrow. I saw success as I thought about the time our tutors gave to our students:

> My flowers need tending
> Weeds are in the way.
> But Ashley is waiting
> To read with me today.

The church called a meeting
I really need to stay.
But Ashley is waiting
To read with me today.

It looks like rain.
The sky is turning gray.
But Ashley is waiting
To read with me today.

—Patricia Oliver

Reflections

School can sometimes be a tough place to implement change, especially with its routines and set practices keeping things the way they've always been. As teachers we never seem to have enough time to meet the needs of all our students—the low and the high, the shy and the headstrong. At the end of a day we find ourselves longing to do a better job, wishing we could clone ourselves. Sometimes we get trapped into thinking that *we* are the only ones who can make the difference. In reality, there is a reservoir of willing minds and bodies just waiting to be asked—people who have the time and the desire to reach out.

Even though the thought of bringing in outsiders to help make change can feel overwhelming, it is our hope and our duty as educators to set up a system of building a community of teachers and learners that exceeds the parameters of our physical buildings. All of this takes time. Time and a change of heart. It takes a paradigm shift.

In all honesty, older people used to scare me with their blue veins and wrinkled skin. I never knew what to talk to them about. They seemed so fragile.

I've changed my mind.

In August of 2003, we were perfect strangers. I'd driven by the retirement facility for ten years, never giving them a moment's thought. But I was plagued by my dilemma of having to find a pool of volunteers to work with our struggling readers and writers. The daunting mandate had declared that no child was to be left behind. Hence, I was desperate and one day as I stopped at the red light, my mental ignition revved up . . . there was our resource . . . right in front of me!

So I sat up straight, shifted my car and my mind, and started to pay attention to that block-long facility, which was a two-minute drive from my elementary school. It was their lunch hour in the dining room of the Memorial City Terrace retirement home. There they sat at their round tables. I saw wrinkled faces with laugh lines, tired hands dipping their forks into the pile of mashed potatoes plunked side by side with baked chicken and green beans on white china plates. Wait staff wandered with jugs of iced tea. Their activity director had allowed me three minutes of airtime during their lunch hour announcements. I spoke in between the news of where to locate the new Bingo cards and when the Wal-Mart run was scheduled for later that day. I could hear forks clanking as I spoke and I wondered what was going on inside their gray-haired heads.

I asked them to raise their hands if their answers were *yes* to the following two questions: "Do you like to read?" and "Do you like children?"

Lots of hands shot up and I saw their eyes twinkle. I let them know that those were the only requirements for them to be a part of our volunteer tutoring program. All I needed was one hour a week from them. I announced that there would be an information session the next day and I looked forward to seeing them tomorrow.

Two hesitant people attended the first informational meeting. Eight came to the subsequent training. Seven months later we were numbering eighteen volunteers. Now they are no longer perfect strangers. They have become my "new old friends." They greet their students with warm hugs every week. And the rippling effects of their involvement will make any heart sing.

Every week like clockwork they arrive. Their bus pulls up to the curb. Very slowly and carefully they exit taking a full two minutes to walk the twenty yards to our community center. Two have walkers, one has a cane. Four of them wear hearing aids. Two hold hands wherever they go. Holding the door open for them, I smile and welcome each one. It's a parade of the most delightful group of souls I've ever encountered.

Up saunters Mr. Fred, a former math professor. In his hand he holds a walrus tusk. Brought it in to share with Andrew as they will be reading about sea animals today. He's wearing the same soft blue turtleneck I complimented him on last week.

Then comes Miss Francis. Always with the minipage of the *Houston Chronicle* to show her limited English speaking student Kenta. When Kenta started he would sit the whole hour and not say a word. Now he chatters freely and scoots his chair as close as physically possible pointing at pictures and identifying words.

Hermann is an ex-pilot. He is a large boisterous man sporting a different favorite baseball hat each week. Hermann's knowledge overflows and he is so eager to share with young Raphael who has no father at home. In his "other" spare time, Hermann dresses as a clown to entertain children at the local hospital's cancer ward.

Before the students arrive, the tutors settle down with their supplies for the day. I pull out an article from the *Houston Chronicle* informing us that the oldest person in the world died last week. "How old?" Alice inquires as she grins that famous toothless Alice grin.

"One hundred fifteen years old—a former shoemaker from Spain," I reply. We all turn to Miss Dottie, the senior member of our tutoring squad. She is really ninety-three, but she whispered into my ear one day that she reversed the digits a long time ago. She's really 39. "Miss Dottie!" I exclaim. "That means you can keep coming for 22 more years!" She blushes and we all clap.

At 10:00 AM sharp the students arrive, bursting through the door making a beeline to their special buddy. This is my time to be a sponge and soak in the magic. They hug. I hear snippets of conversations:

"Hey, how are you doing? How did your vocabulary test go?"
"Wow, you look sharp today . . . great haircut!"
"Sit down and tell me about your week!"

The students span first through fifth grade. Each one is there for a different reason. Some of them are ESL kids, others are at risk for one reason or another. Some need more focus on decoding, others on comprehension. But *all* of them are at ease, eager to be there for this magical hour where they can transcend the other 167 hours of the week.

The hour goes like this:

1. *The tutor shares—the student listens.* The first five to ten minutes the tutor reads aloud something from their world of print. It can be a poem, a newspaper article, a favorite picture book, a chapter, or a photo

album accompanied by a diary entry. This form of sharing "reading in the wild" models how reading is a part of our everyday lives. It's how we learn and how we're entertained. It keeps us thinking!

2. *The student rereads a familiar book.* For the next ten minutes the student shows off and practices fluency reading with expression. The tutor's job is to be wowed and to compliment the student.

3. *New reading material.* The classroom teacher has sent a new book to be covered for the next twenty minutes. Together the tutor and student access schema, do a book walk, make predictions, and then proceed. Throughout the reading they stop to think aloud, make connections, inferences, ask questions, make predictions, and fix up their mistakes. They talk about what they are visualizing as they are reading.

4. *Writing activity.* Choosing from a variety of suggestions, the student follows up the reading with a response.

5. *Sharing time.* The last five minutes of the time is spent with volunteers/ student pairs who wish to share something from the hour. Ardley stands up one day, "I learned today that when a tree is sawed down, you can count the number of rings to learn how many years old it is." Yobani recently shared a poem he wrote. Alice composed a wonderful story that she keeps adding onto each week. (Alice also invited Miss Ruth, ninety-one years old, to her birthday party. Together they shared Chinese food!)

A former dance studio owner, Miss Margo, age eighty-nine, has had the highlight of her year. Today during sharing time she asked if she could teach a little of her ballet knowledge to the group. Most of the students rallied. They learned all of the positions, with accompanying arm movements. She said, "Great! Now all you have to do is smile!" They did and she radiated, just as our assistant principal stepped in to share the moment.

The good-byes are just as goose bumpy as the hellos. Tutors give hugs, a "have a great week," and then students are off. The tutors then write a note to the teacher explaining what they did that day, making observations and asking questions. You can hear a pin drop as they document their time. They hand me their letters and their hour is over. Time for Bingo and the Wal-Mart run.

I escort them to their bus. I board and wish them well, thanking them once again for taking the time to make a difference in a young life.

Then there's Dudley, a former NASA engineer who always wants the last word. He has an announcement. Tonight and tomorrow night we can look up in the sky to see the planets lined up. It won't happen again for another twenty-three years. "That means if you don't get up on our third floor balcony tonight you'll never see it in your lifetime!" He admonishes all of us who like to go to bed early. We smile and nod.

I dare say that no one is being left behind in this program. Not the old, not the young. And now another perfect stranger wishes to join our group. She has a walker and a hearing aid. Nona is her name. Some lucky child at our school is about to have a new "old" friend.

Fellow educators, how can we deprive our students and our willing volunteers of this priceless opportunity? They're just waiting to be asked, and once they say *Yes!*, there is no stopping the momentum. Think about it.

APPENDICES

Brochure–Literacy Tutors

You Can Make a Difference!

As a literacy tutor, you will face many challenges but you will be rewarded with the knowledge that you have given hope and confidence to a struggling reader. You will be making a commitment to helping a student succeed by offering support and encouragement for reading and writing. As part of _____'s Reading Team, you can help turn failure into success!

Literacy Tutors

An Essential Part of _____'s Reading Team! [Your School]

Brochure–Literacy Tutors

To become successful independent readers and writers, students need effective classroom instruction. Many students are able to learn to read and write successfully within the regular classroom. But for students who are not part of the *literacy club*, additional intervention is needed to ensure their success in reading and writing. One of the most effective interventions for students is one-to-one tutoring.

At [Your School], we are dedicated to the goal that every student will become a successful, independent reader. To ensure that success, we are looking for volunteer literacy tutors to become part of _____'s Reading Team!

Training

As a volunteer literacy tutor, you will receive training in reading and writing strategies as well as letter and word work. Follow-up sessions will be conducted throughout the year where you will have the opportunity to hear feedback from the tutoring supervisor and discuss your individual students. You will receive training in several areas: (1) the reading process; (2) what readers do before, during, and after reading; (3) letter and word study; and (4) writing.

The volunteer supervisor will assist you in developing lessons for your students. As a literacy tutor, you will receive handbooks and materials the will ensure your success as a tutor.

When and Where

The tutoring may take place before or after school or during the regular school day. The times will be determined by the tutor and the classroom teacher. We are asking for a commitment of at least two thirty-minute sessions each week. Each thirty-minute session will usually include the following components: (1) ten minutes of reading aloud, reading familiar books or text, and reading the new book or text; (2) five minutes of letter or word work; and (3) fifteen minutes of writing.

A–1 *Continued*

48

Sample Sign for Inviting Tutors to Join

Literacy Tutoring Program at [Your School]

Please ask yourself three questions:

1. Do you love to read?

2. Do you love children?

3. Are you willing to commit to two 30-minute sessions or an hour per week to help a child through May?

If you answered *yes* to all of the above questions, then please come to an information session tomorrow in the Community Room at 10:00 AM to hear the details!

A–2

Volunteer Literacy Tutor Information

Name: _____

Address: _____

Email address: _____

Phone: _____

   Home: _____

   Work: _____

Days and times you'd like to tutor: _____

Grade level preference: _____

Number of students you would like to tutor: _____

Any questions or concerns? _____

_____

_____

Sample Literacy Tutor Schedule

Time	Monday	Tuesday	Wednesday	Thursday	Friday
8:00–8:30		Mr. Smith—Jimmy 2nd Grade—Ms. Jones		Mr. Smith—Jimmy 2nd Grade—Ms. Jones	
8:30–9:00	Ms. White—Mandy 1st Grade—Ms. Wise		Ms. White—Mandy 1st Grade—Ms. Wise		
9:00–9:30	Ms. Green—Bobby 3rd Grade—Ms. Smart		Ms. Green—Bobby 3rd Grade—Ms. Smart		

A–4

Teacher Survey

This year our school is implementing (or continuing) a volunteer literacy tutoring program. Using trained volunteer literacy tutors, students who need additional support for reading will have the opportunity for individualized instruction with a caring, knowledgeable adult. Since the success of any literacy tutoring program is based on the combined efforts of classroom teachers and tutors, your input is vital. Please take a few minutes to complete the following survey.

What do you see as the benefits of a volunteer literacy tutoring program?

_____

_____

_____

What concerns do you have about a volunteer literacy tutoring program?

_____

_____

_____

What do you see as your role in a schoolwide volunteer literacy tutoring program?

_____

_____

_____

Would you want your students pulled out of class to receive one-to-one tutoring? Why or why not? (*Note:* This will not supplant your guided reading program.)

_____

_____

_____

Think about potential students in your classroom. (*Note:* Do not include students in special education, reading recovery, or any students already receiving intervention services.) How would they benefit from having a tutor? What specific things would you like the tutor to focus on during the tutoring session?

_____

_____

_____

Thank you for your input!

A–5 *Continued*

Tutoring Assignment

Dear _____ ,

Your student _____ has been assigned _____.

He/she will be picked up by the tutor on _____ at _____.

Please let me know as soon as possible if the student is absent or will not be available on that day and time.

Thank you for all your support!

Sincerely,

[Literacy Tutor Supervisor]

Sample Letter to Parents

October 25, 200X

Dear Parents,

It is my great joy to tell you about the community bond _____ has established with _____.

Senior citizens from _____ have volunteered to tutor children once a week on Wednesday from 10:00–11:00. Each senior citizen is matched 1:1 with a student to support the language arts skills being taught in the classroom. Students are *not* pulled during their guided reading groups; this support is designed to enrich, not supplant classroom instruction.

Your child is fortunate to be part of this program. Your child's teacher is in communication with the tutor to personalize the time together each Wednesday. If you are free during that time, please drop by and see the program in action!

Needless to say, the learning involved in this cross-generational program is limitless. Research has shown that the senior citizen is the most underutilized resource in our country. It is a win–win situation. The old need the young; the young need the old.

Please contact me with any questions or comments you may have as the year unfolds. It is my personal passion to ensure success for all when it comes to literacy!

Sincerely,

Mary Wheeler
Language Arts
School Improvement Specialist

A–7

Sample Letter to Classroom Teacher

September 26, 200X

Dear _____,

Based on the recommendation of _____, your student _____ has been assigned a trained volunteer literacy tutor. Your student's tutor has spent many hours learning about the reading process and how to provide effective individualized instruction. The time spent with the literacy tutor is designed to support and enrich classroom instruction, so your student will not miss small-group instruction in reading. I know your student will find the tutoring session a rewarding and successful experience. The tutor, classroom teacher, and I will provide ongoing monitoring of your student's literacy development. Feel free to contact me if you have any questions or concerns.

Sincerely,

Patricia Oliver, Ed.D
School Improvement Specialist
Sherwood Elementary

Tutoring Friend Information Sheet

Getting to Know You!

My name: _____

Where I was born: _____

Where I grew up: _____

What I was like in elementary school: _____
_____

My family members: _____
_____
_____

Places I've traveled: _____
_____

Jobs I've had: _____
_____
_____
_____

Books I like to read: _____
_____
_____

Why am I volunteering? _____
_____

Other things I do in my spare time: _____
_____
_____

My heroes: _____

Words people use to describe me: _____
_____

(*Note:* This was sent home to the parents along with a photograph of the tutor and student.)

A–9

Suggestions for Orientation Packet

Include:

- Supervisor's name, school and home phone number, email address

- Map of building

- District and school calendars of events

- Names of teachers and room numbers

- Names of contact people in the building (principal, assistant principal, administrative assistant, counselor, nurse)

- School brochure (if one is available)

- List of materials in the building that are available for the tutors to use

- Calendar showing dates when the supervisor will be out of the building and the name of a substitute contract

Helpful Information Sheet

Teachers: Please fill out one page for each student you are considering for the volunteer literacy tutoring program.

Child's name: _____

Teacher's name: _____

Reading level: _____

Reading strengths:

Reading concerns:

Writing/reading prowess:

What else do we need to know about this student to make this program most successful?

B–1

What to Bring List

First Day of Tutoring Bring:

1. A blank spiral notebook (to be kept in tutorial book box)

2. A familiar reading book (to be kept in tutorial book box)

3. An object of personal meaning to share with the tutor

4. A smile and a grateful heart!

My student(s): _____

Way I'll remember to send them: _____

_____

Coordinating Teacher Responsibilities Worksheet

1. Send your student every _____ at _____ to the community center. Please be punctual!

(If student is absent that day, contact supervisor so tutor can be called.)

2. Write to the tutor every week. Be specific with any skills that need reinforcing. Put this letter in tutor tote _____ of each week!

SPECIFIC SKILL IDEAS: Previewing the text and discussing before reading ~ Predicting ~ Rereading to gain fluency ~ Reading dialogue to gain expression ~ Reading punctuation and emphasizing correctly ~ Summarizing ~ Finding the main idea ~ Specific strategies for identifying unknown words ~ Making connections ~ Identifying author's purpose ~ Making a Y chart to ensure comprehension ~ Use a story chart ~ Word study with prefixes and roots ~ Compound words ~ Contractions ~ Literature responses ~ Comparing/contrasting stories ~ Extension activities

3. Supply *just right* on level reading materials every week.

TEXT IDEAS: Time for kids ~ Scholastic ~ Chapter book ~ Any reading material on the child's instructional level that would support what you are doing in the classroom. Use literacy library materials. These materials become familiar reading and will stay in the students' boxes for a few weeks before being returned to you.

B–3

© 2005 by P. Oliver and M. Wheeler from *A Supervisor's Guide to You Said Yes!* Portsmouth, NH: Heinemann.

Remember!

REMEMBER!!!

_____'s tutoring time is

_____ at _____!

REMEMBER!!!

_____'s tutoring time is

_____ at _____!

REMEMBER!!!

_____'s tutoring time is

_____ at _____!

REMEMBER!!!

_____'s tutoring time is

_____ at _____!

REMEMBER!!!

_____'s tutoring time is

_____ at _____!

REMEMBER!!!

_____'s tutoring time is

_____ at _____!

REMEMBER!!!

_____'s tutoring time is

_____ at _____!

REMEMBER!!!

_____'s tutoring time is

_____ at _____!

REMEMBER!!!

_____'s tutoring time is

_____ at _____!

REMEMBER!!!

_____'s tutoring time is

_____ at _____!

REMEMBER!!!

_____'s tutoring time is

_____ at _____!

REMEMBER!!!

_____'s tutoring time is

_____ at _____!

Note—Supervisor/Tutor

Child's name: _____   Teacher's name: _____

Date: _____   Tutor: _____

Celebrations!

_____

_____

_____

_____

Concerns!

_____

_____

_____

_____

Suggestions?

_____

_____

_____

_____

C–1

Note—Teacher/Tutor

A Note from the Classroom Teacher to the Tutoring Friend!

Child's name: _____   Teacher's name: _____

Date: _____   Tutoring friend: _____

Dear _____,

Today could you please focus on _____

_____

_____

_____

_____

I am noticing that _____

_____

_____

_____

_____

Thank you so much for your help!

_____

Note from the Tutor to the Teacher

Tutoring Friends Communication

Child's name: _____   Tutoring friend: _____

Date: _____

Dear _____,

Today we _____

_____

_____

I am noticing _____

_____

I am wondering _____

_____

I look forward to hearing from you!

_____

Sample Appreciation Assembly Notice

Volunteer Appreciation Assembly

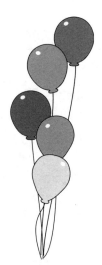

On the hardtop
April 16th, 200X
9:00

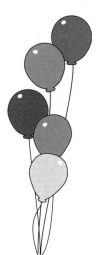

Sample Letter of Appreciation from Supervisor

Letter to My Volunteers

Good morning to my new "old" friends!

Please don't take offense to the word *old*! Because you all have become so important to me. Almost twice my age and as a result, twice as wise and twice as nice. You amaze me every single week with your dedication in our program. And I know I tell you so until you're probably tired of hearing about it. So this week I write you a little note . . . hopefully I'm choosing font large and legible enough to make it a comfortable reading experience for your eyes. Therefore all of your reading energy can be spent on having these words digest directly to your hearts where they belong.

First of all, I want you to go straight home and put this date on your calendar . . . Friday April 16th! Your bus will bring you here for a special volunteer appreciation assembly. You will be greeted by your Wednesday Reading Buddy who will escort you to our celebration where you will have reserved seating. It will last from 9:00–9:45. I hope *all* of you can come!

Next, I wanted to share this story, called "Life and a Cup of Coffee."

Sometimes life feels like too much to handle. Twenty-four hours in a day are just not enough.

And when life feels like this, we are to remember the mayonnaise jar and the coffee. The story goes like this:

> A professor stood before his philosophy class and had some items in front of him. When the class began, wordlessly he picked up a very large and empty mayonnaise jar and proceeded to fill it with golf balls. He then asked the students, "Is my jar full?"
>
> They said, "yes!"
>
> So, the professor picked up a box of pebbles and poured them into the jar. He shook the jar lightly. The pebbles rolled into the open areas between the golf balls. He then asked the students again, "Is my jar full?"

D–2

They said, "yes!"

So the professor got out a bag of sand and poured it into the jar. You can imagine that the sand filled up everything else. Once more he inquired, "Is my jar full?"

It was a unanimous, "yes!"

From under the table the professor brought out two cups of coffee. He poured the coffee into the jar and filled up the empty spaces between the grains of sand. Laughter filled the room.

"Now," said the professor, "my jar is full."

He continued. "This jar represents your life. The golf balls are the important things: your family, your children, your health, your friends, your faith, your passions . . . things that if everything else was lost and any remained, your life would still be full. The pebbles are the other things that matter like your job, your house, your car. The sand is everything else . . . the small stuff. If you had put the sand into the jar first, there would be no room for the pebbles or the golf balls. The same goes for life. If you spend all your time and energy on the small stuff, you will never have room for the things that are important to you. Pay attention to the things that are critical to your happiness. Play with your children and grandchildren. Take time to get medical checkups. Take your cherished friends and family members out to dinner. Play a round of golf. There will always be time to clean the house and fix the garbage disposal. Take care of the golf ball items first—the things that really matter. Set your priorities. The rest is just sand."

One student raised her hand and asked, "What was the coffee for?"

The professor smiled and said, "I'm glad you asked. It just goes to show you that no matter how full your life may seem, there's always room for a couple of cups of coffee with a friend."

That was a long story! But you know why I typed it for you? Because somewhere in the jar of your life, you have decided that coming to [Your School] once a week is a pebble for you. Somehow you are working the other things in. You make a *huge* difference at our school and we all appreciate it more than any words can express.

Enjoy this beautiful spring day and may you have a spring in your step knowing that you are giving us such a gift with your commitment!

Fondly,

Mary

D–2 *Continued*

Invitation to Brunch

You are invited

to a brunch on

—————————————

for literacy tutors

and students!

Please come to

the library between

____ and ____

to celebrate everything

you have accomplished

this year!

Sample Poem from Supervisor to Tutor

Write a personal poem to each volunteer.

> The choir calls me up.
> They need me to stay.
> But _____ is waiting
> To read with me today.
>
> There is work at home
> That won't go away.
> But _____ is waiting
> To read with me today.
>
> I have so much to do.
> It's out of my way.
> But _____ is waiting
> To read with me today.
>
> —*Patricia Oliver*

D–4

A Note of Tutor Appreciation

Some Fall thoughts for Our Marvelous Volunteers!

As I was carving my pumpkin this weekend I thought about all of you. First I took the top off because that's what you do; you open yourselves up to the challenge of working with a needy child.

Then I scooped out all the insides, which is what you do, too! You scoop out all of the things that tangle up their reading and writing so they don't get confused.

You are a new pair of eyes; you have a smile that won't quit, and you have a triangle nose that inhales their thoughts. Most important, you are the light that is put inside. You illuminate with your giving spirit.

Even after this fall season passes, you will be thought of as jack o'lanterns. Glowing and bringing a smile to everyone's face. Thank you so much for your commitment to our school and our children!

—Mary Wheeler

A Sample Letter of Appreciation

November 3, 200X

Dear Special Friends,

Sometimes I think of you as my "Wednesday" friends, but that doesn't work because I think of you seven days a week. You are my friends on Sundays, Mondays, Tuesdays, Thursdays, Fridays, and Saturdays as well as Wednesdays!

So I think of you as my *special* friends. Like no other people in my life. For other than my own mother, who is eighty-eight, I don't really have the opportunity to associate with the older generation. And you know I tell you every week that you are my heroes. You are upbeat, positive, willing, fun loving, and so very wise. Perhaps your ears are getting tired of hearing this, but I never tire of saying it—on Wednesdays or any other day of the week.

So today I'm putting my gratitude in writing so you can read it later! And this message is entirely inspired by the image of carving a pumpkin. This is what you mean to me.

1. *Imagine me taking off the top of the pumpkin.* You, my special friends, open up my heart and mind to things I otherwise would not be exposed to in my elementary school bubble.

2. *Imagine me lifting out all the yucky stringy insides.* When I'm with you, I'm reminded that the yucky unnecessary petty stuff in life clogs up my thinking! It's no good and needs to be eradicated from my life!

3. *Imagine me poking out the precut eyes.* You all give me clarity about what's important in life. I always walk away from your bus with 20/20 vision. Peripheral!

4. *Imagine me poking out the nose.* Because of you, I don't get my nose out of joint. I take time to smell the smells of fall: scented candles, pumpkin pies, and the misty rainy mornings. This lovely season welcomes the holidays.

D–6

5. *Imagine me shaping the mouth.* I listen to your kind and helpful words to your children. I'm reminded of the joy that erupts when encouragement reigns in our world. I want to train my brain to think before my mouth ever opens to say hurtful words. In short, I want to be like you when I grow up.

6. *Imagine me lighting a candle inside the pumpkin.* This is the light *you* bring each week when you leave the Terrace and enter Bunker Hill's parking lot. You encourage *everyone* you see to want to be like you when they reach that dignified stage of life. You radiate joy. You glow. And we *all* love that!

I hear all the time what a wonderful program this is and how incredible you people are to give of your time and your hearts. So rather than wait until Thanksgiving to let you read my gratification, I give it to you today. Maybe your name isn't Jack, so substitute your name _____ 'O Lantern!

See you next Wednesday, my seven-day friends!

Love,

Mary

D–6 *Continued*

Valentine Thoughts

On _____ mornings
it never fails . . .
A (Texas)-sized smile on my heart prevails
For I know that come around 10 o'clock
My incredible tutors arrive in a flock!
Ready for action!
Ready to assist!
Your love of children cannot be missed.
I get to stand back and watch
Your kindness outpour—
And feel the love as you walk
through the door.
You're amazing!
You're fun!
I call you my "HEROES"
—my "CELEBRITIES."
But today you're my Valentines
'cuz it's February!

—*Mary Wheeler*

D–7

Literacy Tutor First-Aid Kit

In a resealable bag, include:

- band-aids: for those rough days with your student

- candies: for those days when you need a little TLC

- a small box of crayons: to see the colors in the world

- a small container of modeling clay: to remind you take time to play

- bookmark: to read something just for fun today

- eraser: to remind yourself that everyone makes mistakes

- a package of seeds: to take time to smell the roses

- penny: for good luck with your student

- paperclip: to help you hold everything together

- rubber band: to help you stretch your thinking

- small bottle of bubbles: to help you take a deep breath and blow out any stress

- minibag of popcorn: to make the smells in the air fun

- heart-shaped candy: because you are always in our hearts

Ideas for a Sweet Thank-You!

Ask your administrative assistant to help you make the following labels to place on each piece of candy. Place the candy in the tutor's mailbox. Or, decorate a basket, fill it with candy, and stand a large sign behind it. Invite tutors to take a sweet thank-you!

- 3-Musketeers: *Thank you for being part of our team!*

- Snickers: *It's okay to laugh. Students say the "darndest" things!*

- Milky Way: *You are stars in our eyes!*

- M&M's: *Magnificent & Marvelous Tutors!*

- Whoppers: *Wow! You're wonderful!*

- Almond Joy: *You are a joy to have at school!*

- Hershey bar: *You are a scrumptious as chocolate!*

- Nestle's Crunch: *You are always here to help us in a crunch!*

- Tootsie Roll: *Thanks for rolling with the punches!*

- Butterfinger: *Thank you for grabbing hold of our readers!*

- Baby Ruth: *Thanks for help us work through the nuts and bolts of reading!*

- Juicy Fruit gum: *Thanks for sticking it out!*

- Smartees: *Thanks for your smart ideas!*

- Payday: *We can never pay you back for all you do!*

D–9

Ideas for Letters from Students to Tutors

Dear Teachers:

Please ask students to write a letter of appreciation to their tutor and use the tutor's name (My tutor Ms./Mr. _____). The following are suggestions that students might include in their letters.

- Write about what they have learned.

- Write about what they have learned about themselves.

- Include interesting facts they have learned about their tutors.

- List some of the things they have enjoyed talking, reading, or writing about.

- Write about how their tutor has helped them become a better reader.

- Include favorite moments or funny stories about the time with their tutor.

Possible letter starters:

- If I could pick any tutor, I would choose you.

- The top ten reasons why I enjoy having _____ as a tutor are . . .

- What would I do without _____?

- The most important thing I have learned from my tutor is . . .

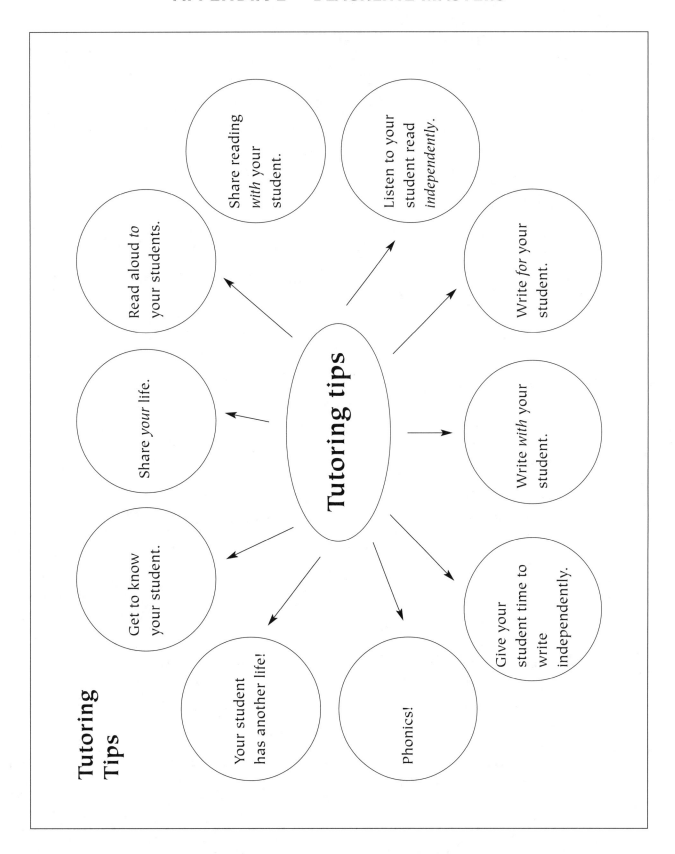

Tutoring Tips

- Share reading *with* your student.
- Listen to your student read *independently*.
- Read aloud *to* your students.
- Write *for* your student.
- Share *your* life.
- Tutoring tips
- Write *with* your student.
- Get to know your student.
- Your student has another life!
- Phonics!
- Give your student time to write independently.

Check the Picture

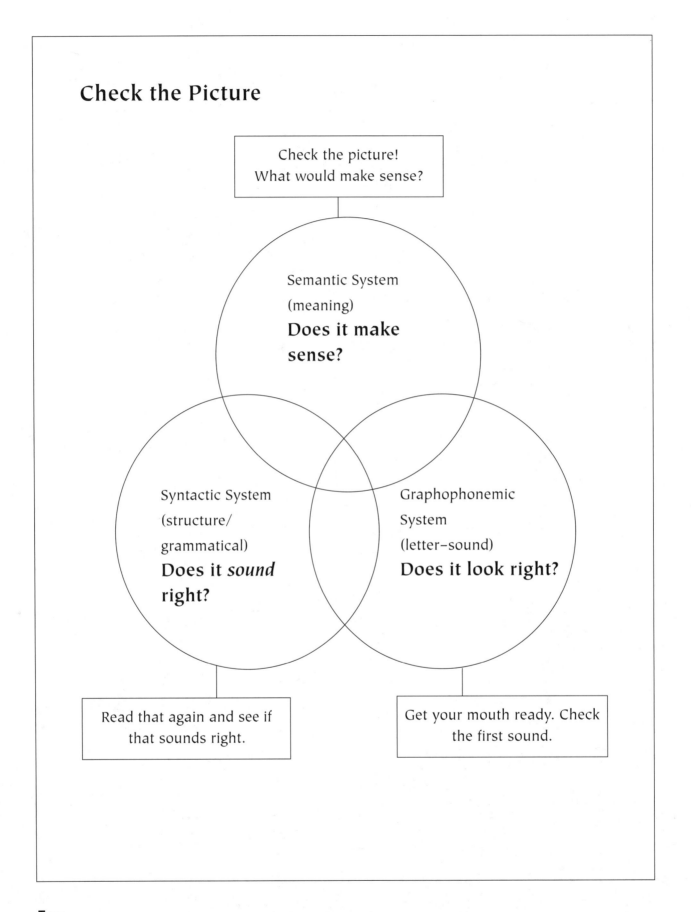

Cueing Information

What cueing or information system do you use to complete these sentences?

Everyone blew out the candles and sang Happy _____.

This is a snuffling. Here are three _____.

The kitten had black, white, and y_____ stripes.

Unknown Words

Some Things to Think About and Do
When You Come to a Word You Don't Know!

Look at the picture!

Think about the story.

Get your mouth ready!

Go back and read it again.

Does it sound right?
Does it look right?

Think:

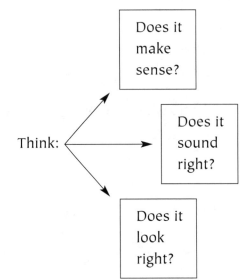

Does it make sense?

Does it sound right?

Does it look right?

Prompts

"Do you know another word that *looks* like that?"	"Do you know another word that *looks* like that?"
"Get your mouth ready. Say the first sound."	"Get your mouth ready. Say the first sound."
"Look at the picture!"	"Look at the picture!"
"Do you remember that word from another page?"	"Do you remember that word from another page?"
"Go to the beginning of the sentence and try it again!"	"Go to the beginning of the sentence and try it again!"
"Sound it out."	"Sound it out."
"Is there a chunk you know?"	"Is there a chunk you know?"
"What would make sense?"	"What would make sense?"

E–5

Reading Strategies

When I come to a word I don't know, I can . . .

• Check the picture.	Cat
• Check the beginning sound.	Kite
• Get my mouth ready.	
• Sound it out.	 "d - o - g"
• Look for parts of the word I know.	*caterpillar*
• Skip the word and come back. (*Will you play a _____ with me?*)	
• Check to make sure it makes sense in the sentence. (*I like to _____ in the rain?*)	

E–6

Book Talk Starters

Book Talk!	Book Talk!
"What connections can you make between what you just read and what you already know?"	"What connections can you make between what you just read and what you already know?"
"Describe what you see in your head while you are reading."	"Describe what you see in your head while you are reading."
"What did you wonder about while you were reading?"	"What did you wonder about while you were reading?"
"What did you figure out about what we read that wasn't in the book?"	"What did you figure out about what we read that wasn't in the book?"
"Please retell in your own words what you just read." 1. 2. 3.	"Please retell in your own words what you just read." 1. 2. 3.
"What did you think was important about what you just read?"	"What did you think was important about what you just read?"

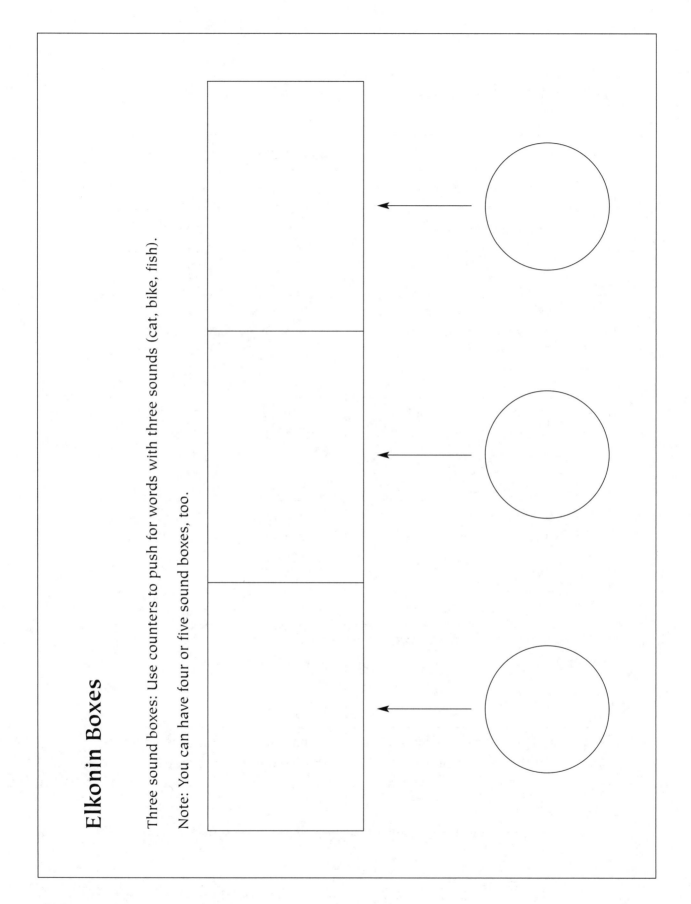

Elkonin Boxes

Three sound boxes: Use counters to push for words with three sounds (cat, bike, fish).

Note: You can have four or five sound boxes, too.

Give It a Try Worksheet

First Try!	Second Try!	Correct Spelling

Suggestions for Making Words

Give the tutors these letters: *i, e, a, y, l, t, r, c.* Ask them to place the letters in one straight horizontal line. This will give them experience in manipulating the letters.

Ask them to

- Use two letters to make the word *it.*

- Change one letter to make the word *at.*

- Add one letter to make the three-letter word *cat.*

- Change one letter to make the word *rat.*

- Add one letter to make the four-letter word *rate.*

- Change one letter to make the word *late.*

- Add one letter to make the five-letter word *later.*

- Put all your letters back in a line. Make the four-letter word *city.*

- Put all your letters back in a line. Make the five-letter word *crate.*

- Can you make a word using all the letters?

(There are other words you can make. Have some fun!)

Individual Word Wall

Aa	Bb	Cc	Dd
Ee	Ff	Gg	Hh
Ii	Jj	Kk	Ll
Mm	Nn	Oo	Pp

Qq	Rr	Ss	Tt
Uu	Vv	Ww	Xx
Yy	Zz	Spelling Patterns	Spelling Patterns
Spelling Patterns	Spelling Patterns	Spelling Patterns	Spelling Patterns

E–11 *Continued*

© 2005 by P. Oliver and M. Wheeler from *A Supervisor's Guide to You Said Yes!* Portsmouth, NH: Heinemann.

Interest Inventory

Name_____   Date_____

Do you have any brothers or sisters? If yes, what are their names? _____

_____

_____

When is your birthday? _____

_____

_____

What are the names of your friends? _____

_____

_____

What do you like to do when you are not in school? _____

_____

_____

What are your favorite foods? _____

_____

_____

Do you have any pets? If yes, what are they? _____

_____

_____

Name three games you like to play. _____

_____

_____

The thing I like about school is _____

_____

_____

When I do things well I like to _____

_____

_____

_____

One thing I hope to learn this year is _____

_____

_____

Elementary Reading Attitude Survey

Name _____

Draw a face to show how you feel.

1. How do you feel about reading at home for fun?

2. How do you feel when the teacher says it is time to read?

3. How do you feel about getting a book for a present?

4. How do you feel about going to the bookstore?

5. How do you feel when the teacher asks you questions about what you read?

E–13

6. How do you feel about reading workbook pages and worksheets?

7. How do you feel when you read out loud in class?

8. How do you feel when your teacher reads out loud to you?

9. How do you feel about reading instead of playing?

10. How do you feel about taking a reading test?

Intermediate Reading Interview

Name _____

1. What do you remember about learning how to read?

2. When you listen to yourself read, what is going on in your head? What are you thinking?

3. Are you still learning to read? Describe how you might be still learning to read?

4. Are there things outside of school you have done that have helped your reading?

5. Tell me about someone you know who is a good reader. What does that person do or what is that person like?

6. How is the good reader you know the same/different than you?

7. What is the single most important thing you know to do if you get stuck on a word? Is there anything else, after that?

8. Teachers spend a lot of time teaching reading. What do you think about that?

9. If you were a teacher, what would you do to help a student who was having trouble reading?

10. Do you think students your age read when they are not in school? How do you think they feel about reading?

11. What kinds of things do you like to read?

12. If an author wrote a book just for you, what kind of book would you like?

Suggested Read-Aloud Books for Tutor Training

Book Title	Author
My Rotten Red-Headed Older Brother Great for modeling thinking aloud and making connections.	Patricia Polacco
When the Relatives Came Use as a springboard for writing. Have the tutors try a quick write about their relatives.	Cynthia Rylant
Mrs. Spritzer's Garden Perfect for starting the first day of training! Hand them a package of seeds as a reminder of the *flowers* they will help to grow.	Edith Pattou
Chrysanthemum Great for modeling thinking aloud and making connections. Every student has been embarrassed or upset about something that happened at school. Good icebreaker—tutors can talk with students about their own names.	Kevin Henkes
Wilfred Gordon McDonald Partridge Good icebreaker—basis for bringing artifact to share during first meeting.	Mem Fox

F–1

Book Title	Author
The Three Questions	Jon J. Muth

Addresses wonderful questions that tutors might ask like, When is the best time to do things? Who is the most important one? What is the right thing to do? Ends with "Remember then that there is only one important time, and that time is now. The most important one is always the one you are with. And the most important thing is to do good for the one who is standing at your side."

| *The Tin Forest* | Helen Ward |

This book has a quiet, yet powerful theme. Sometimes simple ideas can change things. Ideas can turn rain into sunshine. Dreams can make plants grow.

| *The Important Book* | Margaret Wise Brown |

A classic book to share with the tutors. Have them write about the important thing about being a literacy tutor.

F–1 *Continued*

Suggested Read-Alouds—Library

Book Title	Author
Making Connections (grades K–2)	
Arthur's New Puppy	Marc Brown
A Color of His Own	Leo Lionni
Ira Sleeps Over	Bernard Waber
Koala Lou	Mem Fox
My Friend Rabbit	Eric Rohmann
Nana Upstairs, Nana Downstairs	Tomie de Paola
The Snowy Day	Ezra Jack Keats
William's Doll	Charlotte Zolotow
Making Connections (grades 3–5)	
Amazing Grace	Mary Hoffman
Brave Irene	William Steig
The Chalk Box Kid	Clyde Robert Bull
Dinner at Aunt Connie's House	Faith Ringgold
Going Home	Eve Bunting
The Relatives Came	Cynthia Rylant
Drawing Inferences (grades K–2)	
Alexander Who Used to Be Rich Last Sunday	Judith Viorst
Anna Banana and Me	Erik Lenore Blegvad
Corduroy	Don Freeman
In a Small, Small Pond	Pamela Allen
Noisy Nora	Rosemary Wells
Owen	Kevin Henkes
Rainbow Fish	Marcus Pfister
Swimmy	Leo Lionni

F–2

Book Title	Author
Drawing Inferences (grades 3–5)	
Charlie Anderson	Barbara Abercrombie
Once Upon MacDonald's Farm	Stephen Gammell
See the Ocean	Estelle Condra
The Stranger	Chris Van Allsburg
Teammates	Peter Golenback
The Wall	Eve Bunting
Visualizing (appropriate for all grade levels)	
Barn Dance	Bill Martin
Little Mouse's Painting	Diane Wolkstein
Night in the Country	Cynthia Rylant
Owl Moon	Jane Yolan
The Seasons of Arnold's Apple Tree	Gail Gibbons
Seven Blind Mice	Ed Young
The Trip	Ezra Jack Keats
Predictable Books (grades K–2)	
Are You My Mother?	P.D. Eastman
Brown Bear, Brown Bear	Bill Martin
The Gingerbread Boy	Paul Galdone
I Went Walking	Sue Williams
If You Give a Mouse a Cookie	Laura Numeroff
The Important Book	Margaret Wise Brown
Mrs. Wishy-Washy	Joy Cowley
The Napping House	Audrey Wood
The Very Hungry Caterpillar	Eric Carle
More Great Picture Books	
Alexander and the Terrible, Horrible, No Good, Very Bad Day	Judith Viorst
Arthur's Chicken Pox (or any Arthur books by Marc Brown)	Marc Brown

F–2 *Continued*

Book Title	Author
A Chair for My Mother	Vera Williams
A Day's Work	Eve Bunting
Frederick	Leo Lionni
Frog and Toad Are Friends	Arnold Lobel
Ira Sleeps Over	Bernard Weber
Lily's Purple Plastic Purse	Kevin Henkes
The Memory String	Eve Bunting
Miss Nelson Is Missing	Harry Allard
Pink and Say	Patricia Polacco
The Other Side	Jaqueline Woodson
Stellaluna	Janell Cannon
Thank You, Mr. Falker	Patricia Polacco
The True Story of the Three Little Pigs	John Scieszka

Chapter Books

Because of Winn-Dixie (grades 2–5)	Kate DiCamillo
The Best Christmas Pageant Ever (grades 2–5)	Barbara Robinson
Bud, Not Buddy (grades 4–8)	Christopher Paul Curtis
The Cay (grades 2–6)	Theodore Taylor
Charlotte's Web (grades K–4)	E. B. White
Chocolate Fever (grades 1–5)	Robert Smith
Dear Mr. Henshaw (grades 3–6)	Beverly Cleary
A Dog Called Kitty (grades 1–5)	Bill Wallace
Frindle (grades 3–6)	Andrew Clements
Junie B. Jones (grades K–2)	Barbara Parks
The Mouse and the Motorcycle (grades K–3)	Beverly Cleary
Number the Stars (grades 4–7)	Lois Lowry
Soup (grades 4–6)	Newton Peck
Stone Fox (grades 3–5)	John Gardiner
The Stories Julian Tells (grades K–3)	Ann Cameron

Book Title	Author
Poetry Books	
A Bad Case of the Giggles	Bruce Lansky
A Child's Garden of Verses	Robert Louis Stevenson
A Light in the Attic	Shel Silverstein
My Dog Ate My Homework	Bruce Lansky
The New Kid on the Block	Jack Prelutsky
Sometimes I Wonder If Poodles Like Noodles	Laura Numeroff

F–2 *Continued*

Reading Levels Comparison Chart

Guided Reading Levels (Pinnell and Fountas)	DRA (Development Reading Assessment) Levels	Reading Recovery Levels	Stages of Reading
A	A/1	1	Emergent
B	2	2	Emergent
C	3	3 & 4	Emergent/Early
D	4	5 & 6	Emergent/Early
E	6, 7, 8	7 & 8	Emergent/Early
F	10	9 & 10	Emergent/Early
G	12	11 & 12	Emergent/Early
H	14	13 & 14	Early/Transitional
I	16	15, 16, 17	Early/Transitional
J	18	18, 19, 20	Transitional
K	20		Transitional
L	24		Transitional/Fluency
M	28		Transitional/Fluency
N	30		Fluent/Extending
O	34		Fluent/Extending
P	38		Fluent/Extending
Q			Fluent/Extending
R	40		Fluent/Extending
S			Fluent/Extending
T	44		Fluent/Extending
U			Fluent/Extending
V			Fluent/Extending

Note: Check *Guided Reading—Good First Teaching for All Children* by Pinnell and Fountas for a guided reading booklist by levels.

The Swing

How do you like to go up in a swing,
Up in the air so blue?
Oh, I do think it the pleasantest thing
Ever a child can do!

Up in the air and over the wall,
Till I can see so wide,
Rivers and trees and cattle and all
Over the countryside—

Till I look down on the garden green,
Down on the roof so brown—
Up in the air I go flying again,
Up in the air and down!

—Robert Louis Stevenson

My Shadow

I have a little shadow that goes in and out with me,
And what can be the use of him is more than I can see.
He is very, very like me from the heels up to the head;
And I see him jump before me, when I jump into my bed.

The funniest thing about him is the way he likes to grow—
Not at all like proper children, which is always very slow;
For he sometimes shoots up taller like an India-rubber ball,
And he sometimes gets so little that there's none of him at all.

He hasn't got a notion of how children ought to play.
And can only make a fool of me in every sort of way.
He stays so close beside me, he's a coward you can see;
I'd think shame to stick to nursie as that shadow sticks to me!

One morning very early, before the sun was up,
I rose and found the shining dew on every buttercup;
But my lazy little shadow, like an arrant sleepy-head,
Had stayed at home behind me and was fast asleep in bed.

—Robert Louis Stevenson

G–2

Benchmark Education Company
629 Fifth Avenue
Delham, NY 10803
1-877-236-2456
www.benchmarkeducation.com

Heinemann Classroom
Customer Service
6277 Sea Harbor Drive, 5th Floor
Orlando, FL 32887
1-888-454-227
www.heinemannclassroom.com

National Geographic School Publishing
1145 17th Street N.W.
Washington, DC 20036-4688
1-800-368-2728
www.nationalgeographic.com/education

Scholastic Education Leveled Reading
Scholastic Inc.
P.O. Box 7502
Jefferson City, MO 65102-9968
www.scholastic.com/shopleveled

Wright Group/McGraw-Hill
220 East Danieldale Road
DeSoto, TX 75115-2490
1-800-648-2970
www.wrightgroup.com

Cohen, P., C. Kulik, and C. Kulik. 1982. "Educational Outcomes of Tutoring: A Meta Analysis of Findings." *American Educational Research Journal 19* (2):237–248.

Griffith, L. W., and T. V. Rasinski. 2004. "A Focus on Fluency: How One Teacher Incorporated Fluency with Her Reading Curriculum." *The Reading Teacher 58* (2):126–137.

Juel, C. 1996. "What Makes Literacy Tutoring Effective?" *Read Research Quarterly 31* (3):268–289.

National Reading Panel. 2000. www.ed.gov/nclb/methods/reading/reading.hmtl. Accessed July 15, 2002.

Pinnell, G., and I. Fountas. 1996. *Guided Reading—Good First Teaching for All Children.* Portsmouth, NH: Heinemann.

———. 1997. *A Coordinator's Guide to Help American Read.* Portsmouth, NH: Heinemann.

Rasinski, T. V. 2003. *The Fluent Reader.* New York: Scholastic.

Wasik, B. 1997. "Volunteer Tutoring Programs. Do We Know What Works?" *Phi Delta Kappan 78*:282–287.

———. 1998. "Using Volunteers as Reading Tutors: Guidelines for Successful Practices." *Reading Teacher 51* (7):562–570.

Wasik, B., and R. Slavin. 1993. "Preventing Early Reading Failure with One-to-One Tutoring: A Review of Five Programs." *Reading Research Quarterly 28*:179–200.